HEALTHY WITHIN

BRAIN FITNESS
THROUGH NEUROFEEDBACK

BY DIVYA KAKAIYA PH.D., M.S.

HEALTHY WITHIN

BRAIN FITNESS

THROUGH NEUROFEEDBACK

Healthy Within Publications
California

978-1-7346388-0-6
PRINTED IN THE UNITED STATES OF AMERICA

DEDICATION

Without my children, Roshni and Kush, this book would not be.

Without my parents, Paravti and Jagjivan Khatri, I would not be.

Without my brothers, Kishorebhai, Shashikant, and Navin, I would not have had the education.

Without my sisters, Vimlaben, Hemben, and Lattu, I would not have had the confidence to soar.

WITH GRATITUDE

To all my Masters in the field of neuroscience, the pathway each of you created for me in my career has given hope and healing to thousands.

With much gratitude.

To all my patients, who have trusted me for decades and allowed me the Grace of my passions.

TABLE OF CONTENTS

INTRODUCTION

IT IS A WARM, SPRING MORNING and the fourth-grade classroom has completed the morning greeting routine. Mrs. Smith has given the class the assignment that they are supposed to settle into for the next thirty minutes. As the volunteer parent for the classroom, who also happens to be a psychologist, I look around and I see the nine-year-olds squirm in their seats as they settle into the assignment and then hunker down on their desks.

One amazing, bright, young boy who has a very happy smile on his face and a naughty gleam in his eyes intrigues me! You can see that he is very happy to be at school, and *loves* his friends and his teacher. He looks around, pulls his paperwork on his table, pulls out his pencils, and then lo and behold, begins to look around. I am even more enraptured because by now everyone has their heads lowered, and they are writing furiously! He quietly gets up from his table and heads over to the other end of the room to the sharpener. As he saunters over, he looks at his buddies, smiles at them, makes a great connection, and returns to his table with a sharpened pencil!

Luckily for this boy, his teacher has two sons of her own and knows that boys have energy that takes some time to settle in. She watched him carefully without making any comment, realizing that he was distracting a few people along the way, and also that he was about to settle down. He gave her a sheepish grin, and began to do his work in earnest. Mind you, all the other kiddos in his classroom were about ten minutes into their writing.

Wearing two hats in a classroom, a party, or the grocery store has always been a challenge for me. How does one turn off all the years of experience as a psychologist?

It was apparent to me as I watched this little boy that he was on the fringes of extremely "soft," or very mild, signs of ADHD. Even though he wasn't *that* distracting in the classroom by speaking out of turn or interrupting others loudly — and he didn't squirm that much more than a normal nine-year-old boy would — my keen diagnostic eye could see that there was trouble looming ahead.

As this young, bright brain would go into puberty and the hormonal "storms" would bathe his brain, he was going to be very challenged in remaining focused, completing his tasks, and achieving to his potential. The seasoned psychologist in me could not be in denial that this bright young son of ours was going to need some extra support to make sure that his turbocharged brain could serve him well for his entire life.

At this point, I had been practicing for over twenty-four years and knew how vehemently opposed I was to putting our "baby" on medication. So began my journey of finding a holistic treatment that would not include medication. Healthy Within is the treatment center that I founded and run, and in my practice as a psychologist, I am integrative in my perspective. My treatment center was the first one to offer yoga and acupuncture within my specialty, so I knew that I would have to go against mainstream Western treatment to locate what met *our* value system for healthcare.

Conducting an exhaustive search, I came across neurofeedback and after much digging, and to my excitement, we found a psychologist who was just as passionate as I was about how young brains can be healed in much more naturalistic ways.

We embarked on our own journey of taking our son to one whole year of weekly neurofeedback sessions. We saw dramatic changes in his ability to focus, and he was able to zip through his homework in half the time it normally took him. We had obviously drunk the neurofeedback Kool Aid!

With optimism and hope, we saw him sail through puberty, and he remains on task—a focused and very productive member of his high school. Graduating from UC Berkeley is no small feat, and we give a ton of homage to the fact that he was able to create and hold a work ethic that has even landed him his first job post-graduation! Now that my treatment center has become a brain institute, and we have a number of neurofeedback machines at our disposal, I will routinely do "touch-up" sessions on him to ensure his brain solidifies the new neural pathways that we created with the one year of treatment.

Of course, his socialization is still very much like his mother's, except now he is able to complete his tasks and then enjoy his playtime—oops… hanging-out time, now that he is a young man! His ability to remain on task, not be distracted, and complete his work in a timely manner continues to hold up well. As I contemplate the personal and professional journey that has been a part of the treatments we cultivate at Healthy Within, I am grateful for the opportunities that have been available.

Little did I know that rewiring his brain was going to have such a beneficial effect all the way into his college and work career. We did not have a moody teen on our hands, nor did I have to battle about things he needed to get done. He remains a well-regulated young man who is on a path to a meaningful, purposeful career. He is that son who became an Eagle Scout, went to Berkeley, and is the "psychologist" with his group of buddies from college. What more could a parent ask for? A kind, altruistic, well-respected, hardworking, and well-loved son.

My daughter, Roshni, deserves a ton of credit for the feminist brother she has so diligently created. We had no clue that he was going to develop the capacity to create detailed Excel sheets and remain so diligent with his work ethic. As his family, we are incredibly grateful for this path of neurofeedback that was opened to us and allowed Kush to soar to his highest self.

With COVID-19 being such a reality in today's world, and my daughter being a physician on the front lines in her hospital, she is experiencing the acute trauma of being an essential worker. At one point, she reached out to me and wanted me to do a neurofeedback session on her; her brain was so hijacked by the tension that her sleep was profoundly affected. I came into the office on a Sunday and conducted a session on her. She immediately self-regulated and was so much better just after one session.

The symptoms that many long haulers of COVID-19 are experiencing are treatable by neurofeedback. Migraines, pain all over the body, sleep disturbances, and tremors are all treatable by neurofeedback.

Life has brought some incredible gifts to me. Being tricultural is definitely not one of the adjectives I had planned on describing myself with when I was living my happy, content, joyful life in Kenya. I straddled two cultures then since I was of Indian origin and living in an African country. I have early recollections of deciding to be a psychologist when I was about twelve years old. Any types of injustices or imbalances were horrifying to me. Nairobi, the city I grew up in, tended to have a trash collection cycle that was highly irregular. I recall coming up with plans within the community to where we could collectively organize a more methodical system that was going to make our homes more sanitary as well as to organize the city. Little did I know that the roots of my activism were being born right there!

Families are tremendous in the way in which they teach us to have a self and a voice, and to nurture the drive and passion we create. Being raised in a traditional Indian family where the women don't work, independence and a drive to cultivate my own identity became of paramount importance to me. My parents always encouraged any opportunities we created and supported us in any drives that we cultivated.

Academics were highly regarded in our family, and my parents made sure that all the children were adequately equipped to have economic self-sufficiency. My dad in particular wanted to make sure all his daughters could have skill sets that allowed us to support ourselves. He was a moral, righteous, fair man, and my mom was bright, loving, emotionally validating, and incredibly encouraging. Being the youngest of seven ensured that many mothers raised me, and so the idea of nurturing a community was a natural extension of the comfortable, attached environment I came from.

My siblings loved the activist in me, and would often tease me about my social activism! Little did I know that I was going to become an equally active community psychologist who was going to give back to her community in a big way!

Currently, one of the biggest joys I have is the outspoken way in which I empower girls, boys, and families to take back their power from the tyranny of mass media. I run two successful programs, Full of Ourselves and The Boys Council, which are health promotion programs that help young teens have a stronger sense of self and a voice that is not dominated by mainstream media. These programs are run at no cost or very low cost, and I trained about 20 to 25 undergraduates and high school interns who facilitate these groups for Healthy Within.

As I look back, the events that have shaped the intense desire I have to understand the complexities of the brain come from a couple of extremely difficult losses that were monumental for me.

A cousin who was gay was so severely ostracized by the family that his hopelessness gave way to suicide. He was very bonded with our family and we were a sanctuary for him. He had bipolar illness and an eating disorder, as I later came to realize. Growing up in a homophobic Indian culture in the mid-1970s in Kenya was such a losing battle for my poor cousin that he did not have a fighting chance at being able to create a safe space for his identity to blossom.

This senseless loss is one that I still try to come to grips with, hence my driving passion for having families understand mental illnesses from a "brain condition" perspective. Honoring the electrical activity of the brain has become a huge passion of mine. In our practice, we are very clear about the usage of our terms. What I treat at Healthy Within are brain conditions, not necessarily mental illnesses. We still live in such a culture of stigma that I believe that when I liken OCD, anxiety, or depression as a brain condition, very similar to kidney conditions or lung conditions, it helps families understand the instabilities in the brain as organic conditions, which is what they are. Particularly important is my explanation that just as the heart is driven by electrical impulses, so is the brain.

Secondly, when I worked at a short-term psychiatric facility as a graduate student, a patient there committed suicide. I was the only person she left a letter for. At that stage in my life, I had no understanding of alcoholism; she had drunk a six-pack of beer prior to shooting herself.

Being the natural problem-solver and driven person that I am, I immediately began to search out how to deal with addictions and embarked on a twenty-seven-year love affair with treating addictions, eating disorders, substance abuse, adult children of alcoholics, and sexual trauma survivors. This crucial work has been incredibly gratifying; the main pieces that I have connected together through all this work are the genetics and hard wiring of the brain.

I believe that if we had done neurofeedback on her while we were treating her depression, she would likely be alive today. The dilemma of the facility I worked at was that because it was a mental health and psychiatric facility, and not funded by the Department of Alcohol and Drugs, we could not treat the alcoholism—only the depression. Isn't this a crazy way to split the brain? All of what we experience in the realm of sadness, overthinking, insomnia, worry, and so on are all really brain conditions—why can't we treat these from a more holistic perspective?

As my career progressed and I reached the pinnacle of my success with eating disorders, there were subgroups of patients who were incredibly challenging and were an enigma to many of us in the field. The majority of these women were incredible souls, and they were so tormented by their compulsions that I knew there had to be some better avenues of care that we were lacking and that we needed to explore.

When we began to look at neurofeedback, I was incredibly intrigued and wondered whether the neurofeedback research I was reading seemed too good to be true. How could this simple method of "nudging" the brain produce such tremendous results? And why had no one had ever spoken about neurofeedback during the course of my education?

As I dug further into the research studies, I came face to face with the power of the big pharmaceutical companies. If the field of neurofeedback had even 20 percent of the ads that are carried by big pharmaceutical companies, more people would be choosing it automatically! Who really wants *all* the side effects of all the SSRIs and the addictions to the benzodiazepines that naturally come about the minute you start to take any of them?

Having worked in the field of eating disorders and seeing the toxicity that is carried via the virus of the media, I have become increasingly alarmed at the manner in which our country is becoming medicalized. We have become highly skilled at identifying symptoms and making a drug for it. A pill is always available for any ailment, and trying to get to the underlying causes has become a lost cause.

The rapid industrialization of food has created starvation in the brain even as people are getting fatter. We are overfed and undernourished. Autoimmune conditions such as obesity, fibromyalgia, and cancers are epidemic, and we seem to be oblivious to the fact that all these are conditions arising from the dysregulation of the brain. As I began to see the rapid, positive results with some of my most complicated patients, it became apparent that I had hit a jackpot with neurofeedback.

The neuroplasticity of the brain fascinates me and being a practitioner of mindfulness and an avid follower of all meditation traditions, I knew that the unchartered territory of neurofeedback is going to be the next wave of the healing paradigm. My passion about the brain has translated to the vast numbers of presentations I do for psychologists, therapists, school counselors, parents, and teens about the workings of the brain.

Not surprisingly, "The Teen Brain" presentation is the one that is requested the most. I would not feel as comfortable as I do in these presentations if I had not received the Post-Doctoral Masters of Science in Pharmacology. My excitement about natural, holistic treatments increased as the classes progressed and we extensively discussed drug inter-actions and side effects.

Meanwhile, my neurofeedback patients were getting bet-ter, and they no longer needed as much psychotherapy or medications. I often joke with my patients that I am rapidly putting myself out of a job, and then I get discouraged again because there are so many dysregulated brains still awaiting treatment.

The excitement of this field continues to increase, and I hope that my story and discoveries about neurofeedback will reflect the immense power of the brain to heal itself. Af-ter all, we all want to feel happy, content, and calm.

CHAPTER 1

BRAIN 101

*What flows through your mind sculpts your brain,
thus you can use your mind to change your
brain for the better.*

~ Rick Hanson

AS AN AGENT OF WORLD PEACE, the Dalai Lama has partnered with neuroscientists in an exciting endeavor to reveal the secrets of the brain. Happy, successful people seem to know how to harness their brain circuitry to maximize their potential and achieve their goals. These people seem to have "super brains" that have resiliency, as well as the ability to break out of bad habits and continually reinvent themselves.

These next two decades will be the golden era of the brain. Our knowledge of the brain in the 1970s and 1980s was minimal compared to what has emerged in these past five to eight years. Never has it become clearer to us that how we train the brain really creates the outcomes we want and desire in life. We are all in awe of the power of this little three-pound organ.

We have been trained to think that once the brain had formed, we were stuck with it—hence the dogma of the unchanging brain. Now, we have the thrilling knowledge that this little organ with its 100 billion nerve cells is capable of being molded by us. This ability for the brain to change, heal, and repair itself is called neuroplasticity. Meditation, brain training, and neurofeedback are all exciting frontiers that can help us create efficient, turbocharged brains that can give us the result of calm, peace, and joy!

Brain Basics

One of the easiest ways of understanding the brain is by looking at the evolutionary process. When life began about 3.5 billion years ago, the basic building blocks were the neural tissue, which slowly developed to become the brain, the CEO of the body. Wouldn't it be a novel concept to treat our brains with the same respect with which we treat the CEO of our company? Evolution continued to build on existing structures, leading to the various parts of the brain: reptilian brain, limbic brain, and neocortex.

The reptilian brain is the most primitive structure of the human brain. This part is the origin of the fight-or-flight response and helps us survive the most dangerous situations. Our survival has depended on us being able to read the threats in our environment with appropriate actions.

Another way to interpret a threat is to see it as a signal that is encouraging us to restore equilibrium before things get out of control. This part of our brain is the one that gives us panic, fears, phobias, and alarms. This "call" is there to mobilize us to get ourselves into balance. This reptilian brain is also called the amygdala, or the emotional brain.

The body feels the threat, and the sympathetic nervous system (SNS) reacts by bathing the brain with cortisol to prepare us to fight. The muscles become tense and alert, and the thalamus sends the wakeup call that sends epinephrine throughout the brain. The epinephrine increases the heart rate, and we can feel our heart pounding in our ears.

Arousal of the SNS is not good for our body at all because all that cortisol and adrenaline suppresses the immune system, emotions intensify, and the body is becoming more hardwired to react to danger. Being cut off on the freeway can also cause this entire reaction. As our limbic system is activated, the prefrontal cortex (PFC), the part of our brain that performs logical thinking, planning, and organization, is shut down. Our ancestors had real, immediate dangers that they need to avoid. Now, the pace of our life is such that we are constantly on the go and secreting tons of cortisol all day long.

This life on slow burn creates brain conditions such as chronic fatigue, cancer, heart disease, obesity, and even diabetes, which is an autoimmune condition. A body and brain under chronic stress are bound to experience wear and tear that can show up within a number of systems such as the gastrointestinal system, where we see rapidly increasing rates of celiac disease, ulcers, colitis, irritable bowel, Crohn's disease, and severe gluten intolerances.

The flu pandemics that occur all over the world are clear indications that the ecology of the human body seems to be imbalanced and in disharmony. Within the realm of reproductive and sexual health, we see increasingly higher rates of infertility coupled with erectile dysfunction, lowered libido, and severe premenstrual syndromes. As we address young women, ovarian cysts and polycystic ovarian syndrome (PCOS) are conditions that seem to be appearing in medical annals with increasing frequency.

Furthermore, an explosion of autism spectrum conditions is the focal point of numerous disciplines, including neuroscience and behavioral medicine. Clearly, there are some health conditions that modern-day stresses appear to be triggering in the brain.

Moving through the physical conditions, as we examine the mental conditions, this hyperaroused, accelerated lifestyle is taking a toll on our psyches. As a psychologist and neuroscientist who has been treating brain conditions for the last 28 years, the most frequent concern that we treat at our clinic is anxiety. Children as young as six years of age are coming in droves as they worry about parents dying, friends being mean to them, and needing to do repetitive rituals to calm themselves. These states of anxiety and panic were not seen twenty years ago.

A region of the brain called the hippocampus is significantly affected by anxiety. The stress hormone, cortisol, running through the brain weakens the neuronal connections and makes the brain a less efficient organ. The hippocampus also helps us store memories, which is why impairment of memory accompanies anxiety. An amped-up amygdala coupled with a weak hippocampus can make a person feel very upset all the time — and not know why they are so upset.

A second psychological effect of the overaroused SNS system is a depressed mood. For a person to feel alert, aroused, and happy, they need a certain amount of norepinephrine. Cortisol, the evil stress hormone, depletes norepinephrine, which can cause someone to feel apathetic and unable to focus or concentrate.

Over time, cortisol begins to reduce the amount of dopamine that is produced in the brain. Dopamine is the feel-good chemical that we experience when we have gone on a rollercoaster. This is also the chemical that is secreted when people get a high from drugs, sex, or food. High amounts of cortisol deplete how much dopamine becomes available for us, which is why people start to do extreme behaviors under stress to get the dopamine rush.

Perhaps one of the more significant ways in which stress impacts the brain is that it reduces serotonin—the neuro-transmitter that helps us maintain a good mood. That feeling of wellness, joy, and buoyancy we have comes from a nice bath in serotonin. Think about the sense of well-being we have after that Thanksgiving turkey dinner! Turkey is rich in tryptophan, which is a precursor to serotonin. Serotonin also drops the level of norepinephrine, so the combined drop makes a person feel blue, less alert, and much less interested in the world. That does not make for a happy being.

However, it is not all bad news in the brain department! In addition to the CNS, we also have tons of control over the parasympathetic nervous system (PNS). This system teaches our body how to relax and rest—it is definitely our friend. In his book *Buddha's Brain,* Rick Hanson calls this system "the rest-and-digest system" as opposed to the fight-and-flight system of the SNS.

PNS and SNS act like a seesaw—when one goes up, the other goes down. The implications of this relationship are huge. Anything we can do to increase the activity of the PNS would wash out the flooding cortisol from the body. So, that five-minute breath break can flush a ton of cortisol out of your system. Even though work may seem too demanding to leave for five minutes, just stepping away and chatting about something light and funny with a co-worker could mean you just added days to the life of your brain and reduced your aging process.

The PNS settles and calms the mind down. Neurofeedback does the same thing that a 40-year veteran of meditation would do, which is to reduce the beta waves and increase the alpha and theta waves. Neurofeedback cools the fires of the SNS and activates the PNS.

Among military veterans, the hyper-aroused hippocampus creates some very specific syndromes — anxiety, the inability to relax, hypervigilance, and nightmares. Most psychologists working with veterans and active-duty military have incorporated neurofeedback as a standard part of the treatment regime due to its beneficial, long-lasting results.

The key to wellness is to find a healthy balance, one where there is just the right amount of stress to alert the system, while keeping a balance of which hormones flood through. The PNS and CNS can be trained to work in a harmonious way with each other. All too often, we let stress take over and don't give ourselves time to relax, let alone make relaxation a priority.

As we improve our understanding of the entire brain, some key parts of this mysterious organ are helpful for us to make friends with in order to truly understand how neurofeedback affects the brain. Three regions of the brain will help us understand the organ more easily: the prefrontal cortex (PFC), anterior cingulate cortex (ACC), and insula.

The prefrontal cortex sets goals, makes plans, organizes, creates action plans, and balances pros and cons. In Neurofeedback Brain Training, this is one of the most prominent regions we train when there is impulsivity and any type of compulsive behavior. These could be behaviors such as Internet addiction, Facebook or other social media addiction, shopping, gambling, cycling, alcohol, and exercise. People with attention deficit disorder are some of our most successful patients. The emotional brain, also known as the limbic brain, becomes well-regulated when we train the PFC. Feelings and thoughts have to be integrated in some way so we can function in a harmonious way in the world.

The anterior cingulate cortex is the part of the brain that helps us integrate thoughts and feelings. A 2012 study conducted by Tang and Posner showed that there were distinct increases in the gray matter of the brain for a group of participants who were enrolled in an eight-week meditation program. Some functions of the ACC are in the areas of the ability to resolve conflict, attention, sustained motivation, and the ability to modulate thoughts and feelings.

Neurofeedback is a clear modality that boosts the connectivity of the neurons in the brain. It produces results such as improved clarity of focus, an increased ability to describe emotions, improved attentiveness to emotions, and being able to attune with them. When the amygdala in the brain is well-regulated, there isn't an erratic flood of emotions. One of the benefits of neurofeedback is that it balances out the activity of the amygdala and creates a calmer brain. A calmer brain becomes a well-regulated mind.

The insula is the part of the brain that is not often talked about yet is one of the most power-packed part of our brain. The prune-sized insula has been long neglected. In recent years, it has emerged as crucial to understanding what it feels like to be human. The initial understanding about the insula only came about because we didn't have imaging techniques that can look into the deep recesses of the brain. Now we have techniques that allow us to see the deeper regions of the brain. The insula gives birth to social emotions such as lust and disgust, pride and humiliation, guilt and atonement.

An article in the *New York Times* gives a good understanding of the insula. Most importantly, the insula gives rise to moral intuition, empathy, and the capacity to respond emotionally to music. It senses the internal states of our body like gut feelings, hunger, and cravings. Our ability to identify our breath and regulate our own breathing patterns is controlled by the insula. The insula is located in the temporal lobes of the brain.

Other functions that the insula controls are the regulation of our blood pressure, pain modulation, receptors for hunger and fullness, homeostasis of the body, a sense of body awareness, and body ownership. The insula also plays a pivotal role in our body's immune response.

Dr. Paulus at the University of California at San Diego reports that the insula "lights up" in brain scans when people crave drugs, feel pain, anticipate pain, empathize with others, listen to jokes, and are shunned in social situations. Sandra Blakeslee's February 6, 2007, article in the *New York Times* describes the impact of the insula in an extremely clear and powerful way. The insula is one of the most important regions of the brain. Damage to the insula can lead to apathy, loss of sexual feelings, and an inability to tell fresh food from rotten food.

The insula is a receiving zone that reads the entire physiology of the whole body. As it does this, it generates subjective feelings that bring about actions like eating, which keeps the body in a state of internal balance. Information from the insula is transmitted to other brain structures that are involved in decision-making. So, if you train your brain with neurofeedback, then you are strengthening your insula. This means that you will develop a deeper connection with yourself, your feelings, and your thoughts. Might this be a key to cultivating a winner's brain?

The wiring of the insula is such that it receives information from receptors in the skin and internal organs. These receptors are receiver cells that specialize in different senses. They are able to detect heat, cold, itching, pain, taste, hunger, thirst, muscle aches, visceral sensations, and the need to breathe. The sense of touch and body position are routed differently.

Dr. Craig, a researcher from the Barrow Neurological Institution in Phoenix, described the details of this circuitry. All mammals have this circuitry to read their body conditions. However, human beings have a brain that has evolved to do a lot more. They have an ability to pick up more signals from the gut, heart, lungs, and other internal organs. These extra signals are then routed to the front part of the insula, especially on the right side, with these sensations being transformed to social emotions.

A bad taste or smell is sensed in the frontal insula as disgust. A sensorial touch from a loved one is transformed into delight. One can see how important this new discovery has been for us neuroscientists. The frontal insula senses love and hate, empathy and contempt, gratitude and resentment, approval and disdain, guilt and remorse, truthfulness and deception.

Researchers have found that people who are better at reading these signals in the insula score higher in tests of empathy. Once can only imagine the cells of the insula that are being damaged as a teen plays violent video games! Or alternatively, the increased connectivity that is fostered when one meditates regularly.

A second modification that is done in the human insula is a type of cell called VEN, Von Economo neurons, named after the scientist who discovered them. Scientists are still trying to understand these VEN cells better. What they do know is that these cells turn feelings and emotions into actions and intentions. Isn't that amazing that we are discovering actual cells that turn emotions into actions? Imagine the implications of that with us being able to achieve the full potential that we are hungry for!

The human insula helps us prepare for events that are about to happen. This anticipation of events to come is a way in which we have been able to get to the top of the food chain. Preparation and anticipation can aid in survival. Additionally, the insula is the same part of the brain that is triggered when a drug addict is confronted with the sights, sounds, smells, or situations that are associated with drug use.

The neural pathways that are created with frequent use makes the brain believe that the only way in which it can survive is to have the same effect of the drug over and over again. This is the reason why one of the most effective behavioral interventions used by Alcoholic Anonymous is for the alcoholic or drug addict not go to the same bar or to get rid of the phone numbers of their sources.

When a drug is given to an addict, it activates the reward system in the brain. What makes the person go back to the drug is the craving. Neurofeedback as a treatment method is a powerful way to reduce cravings in general because it strengthens the insular activity and deactivates the craving brain.

Brain training via neurofeedback has become one of the most successful strategies that alcohol and drug treatment facilities are using to reduce and remove cravings. The majority of the chemical dependency facilities have become very clear about the fact that the addict's brain benefits tremendously from rewiring the circuitry.

Janet is a twenty-two-year-old patient who worked with us using neurofeedback for a range of addictions, severe depression, anxiety, and flashbacks from sexual trauma she had experienced in college. Within six neurofeedback sessions, all her flashbacks were gone! Her psychiatrist had referred her to us since none of the medications were helping with her bipolar depression, addictions, and flashbacks.

Within one month of completing her neurofeedback sessions, she had quit smoking and reported no cravings at one month of smoking cessation. Her moods were much better after one month of treatment three times a week. Additionally, she reported sleeping through the night without any medications, and her mood had improved dramatically.

When Janet came to us, she was at the worst she had ever been and was willing to try anything that could help alleviate her flashbacks. She had been a regular smoker of cigarettes and marijuana as a way to cope with her anxiety — and particularly to alleviate the panic from the flashbacks of the trauma. She did not even have a goal of quitting pot; however, all her cravings subsided and she quit on her own. She did pick up smoking again after about a whole year of not smoking. She recently returned for a tune-up and after the first session, she was back to having quit again. She reported hating the smell of smoke and that her desire for smoking was completely gone again.

Her brain clearly was willing to be rewired, and it's interesting to note that her mood has remained stable. She hasn't taken any medications for mood regulation, nor has she taken any of her ADHD medications for almost two years now. Needless to say, her psychiatrist has continued to refer many of her medication-resistant patients to us.

The thalamus, the central relay system for sensory information, is another part of the brain that it's important to become friends with. This area is located at the brainstem and is buried deep in the cerebral cortex, which we'll also discuss.

The thalamus is a regulator of sensory information and movement — the "switchboard" of information pathways in the brain. It directly connects the internal regions of the brain with the outer layer of the brain. What is important to know is that it also controls the sleep and wake states of consciousness, which determines our level of alertness. Damage to the thalamus can lead to a coma.

This thalamic region is greatly affected by neurofeedback, and our patients report states of arousal as the most immediate effect of the treatment. The thalamus is connected to the hippocampus, which is the memory center of the brain. In humans, the genetic variation of the SSRI transporter system affects the thalamus. People who have this genetic variation tend to have a functionally larger thalamus and are more prone to major depression, PTSD, and suicide.

The hypothalamus, on the other hand, is another completely separate part of the brain that is located just below the thalamus. This part of the brain is responsible for feeling, arousal, our sexual behavior, and the regulation of body temperature. The hypothalamus is extremely important in the role of pleasure and reward. This is the organ that activates the SNS (sympathetic nervous system), the calming part of our nervous system that we discussed earlier in this chapter.

The hypothalamus and pituitary gland work together in unison to produce cortisol, oxytocin, and dopamine. If those reward systems are not activated enough, they make the brain go to extreme addictive behaviors to pump up the feel-good chemicals. Cortisol, dopamine, and oxytocin are three of the most studied neurochemicals within the brain. All these neurotransmitters play an important role in how we respond to stress and tension in our worlds.

In my presentations with teens, the molecule I really want them to understand is dopamine, since that is *the* molecule of addiction. If we are able to teach our teens how to navigate the world of dopamine without resorting to any drugs or addictive behaviors, then we have successfully saved a brain from an addiction.

Neurotherapy resets the circuitry in the hypothalamic region so that the brain is receiving adequate stimulation for the reward system. Any intervention that calms the brain down will have a tremendous effect on reducing the fight/flight response that can be activated by the hypothalamus. A particular form of NFB training called the Alpha/Theta protocol has been highly successful with alcoholics and drug addicts.

Furthermore, people who have experienced trauma in their lives have highly activated CNS systems, and the Alpha/Theta protocol is one of the most soothing protocols for people with histories of trauma. A recent patient at our clinic is a Vietnam veteran who hasn't slept through the night for forty years. His neurofeedback treatment consisted primarily of Alpha/Theta and after six sessions, he began to sleep through the night and ceased having flashbacks from the war.

Neurofeedback is a therapeutic treatment technique that is noninvasive, minimally intrusive, and gentle. It does not create any negative side effects that more aggressive interventions could have. Understanding the other parts of the brain helps one really grasp what an amazing organ we have between our ears!

CHAPTER 2

BRAIN TRAINING AND NEUROFEEDBACK

*The principal activities of brains are
making changes in themselves.*

~ Marvin L. Minsky

NEUROFEEDBACK TRAINING (NFT) is a learning technique by which the brain improves its function by receiving information about its own brainwaves. The brain can be encouraged to produce more or less of certain brainwaves by the simple feedback of music, audio tones, visual feedback, and tactile feedback. If we have too many waves of a certain frequency or too few of another, then we have unwanted, undesirable symptoms.

Neurofeedback enhances the brain's communication network in a painless and noninvasive way. Areas that are functioning poorly can move toward normalcy. Areas that are functioning well can be brought to an even better level of functioning, which is why we use neurofeedback for peak athletic performance and to increase productivity in the workplace. In numerous cases, neurofeedback has reduced the client's need for medication.

Words that are interchangeably used for neurofeedback are neurotherapy, neurofeedback training (NFT), brain training, brain biofeedback, or brain EEG biofeedback. Research in this field has grown exponentially in the last twenty years, with numerous controlled studies showing significant positive outcomes for neurotherapy. Practitioners who conduct neurofeedback can be psychologists, Master's level therapists, nurses, psychiatrists, naturopathic doctors, neurologists, and certified neurofeedback practitioners.

Neurofeedback has been around for almost forty years. Nevertheless, most medical schools and graduate schools of psychology in the United States still do not have any courses teaching doctors and psychology students EEG biofeedback. In much the same way, most medical schools still do not have any courses on basic nutrition.

Pharmacology has taken hold of our culture, and major drug companies spend billions of dollars in marketing their medications. Our brains are regulated via biochemistry and electrical activity. By teaching the brain to observe itself and by providing some alternative waves that can regulate it, the brain becomes an organ that knows how to heal itself. Our bodies can be miraculous when we give them the healing path to follow.

To illustrate brain training, imagine that we are learning to ride a bicycle with better balance. Many of us live life riding that bicycle in the sand; neurofeedback guides us to take that bicycle onto a bike path and to ride it more efficiently and smoothly. Once we have learned how to ride a bicycle, we never forget it. Once a brain becomes regulated via neurofeedback and is functioning at its best, happiest self, it knows how to get there by itself.

One of the biggest hurdles a brain encounters is when it gets stuck in survival mode as a result of trauma, depression, or anxiety. Some brains are under-aroused, others are over-aroused, and many brains are highly sensitive and react to the smallest of triggers. Neurofeedback allows the brain to become unstuck and start the self-healing process. It allows the various parts of the brain to communicate with each other more effectively so that the whole brain becomes much more regulated. When the brain is regulated, calm, and focused, the body falls into its natural state of health.

A better functioning brain will have improved sleep patterns; if the brain is getting good, quality sleep, then it knows how to regulate itself in other areas too. Most sleep medications interfere with REM (rapid eye movement) sleep, which is a very deep and restful level of sleep so the brain is able to produce the fifty chemicals that it makes when we sleep! The brain also needs its "fifty shades of sleep!"

When a person sleeps well, they are more alert during the day, the depression lifts, and anxiety is reduced. The overall sense of wellness can translate to fewer headaches and migraines, and less of a need to do compulsive behaviors in order to numb the distress. The parasympathetic nervous system, the one that teaches us to rest and relax, is nudged to start functioning for us so we can move out of the fight-or-flight zone.

Neurofeedback helps by first understanding where the irregularities are in the brain via the EEG and then, with the help of a trained practitioner, the brain will be guided to a more efficient place. When we think about how much the brain is processing consciously and unconsciously at any given moment, we can see how the neural circuitry is in a dynamic state.

When conscious or unconscious processing efficiency becomes compromised through the stress of modern living, information overload, trauma, or other influences, loss of performance and suffering arises. The body systems it regulates are affected, processing and integration of life experience becomes inefficient, and the additional burden placed on the conscious mind results in loss of awareness and performance in the world. Consequently problematic behaviors, ill health, and dependencies arise.

All of these processes are affected by the central nervous system, resulting in:

- difficulty concentrating
- fatigue
- impaired mind-body coordination
- impaired hand-eye coordination
- learning difficulties
- difficulties maintaining focus and concentration
- poor response times
- difficulty with decision-making
- reduced problem-solving capacity
- emotional difficulty
- poor coping skills
- cognitive instability
- personality instability
- reduced physical health
- cognitive decline
- rigid beliefs
- diminished personal power
- loss of sense of self
- poor impulse control

- reactivity
- lack of adaptability
- loss of clarity
- sleep disturbances
- overall poor coping strategies

Neurofeedback treatment can only be efficacious if there is a holistic perspective. One has to account for the fact that the brain is one of many organs in the body, and balance needs to be there—just like with other parts of the body with such nutrition and exercise as well. If neurofeedback is being conducted and after an extensive set of treatments, certain imbalances remain, then one must examine the food chain and where there may be hormonal or other nutritional deficiencies.

Our treatment team will often consist of a psychologist, neurotherapist, nutritionist, psychiatrist, medical doctor, acupuncturist, chiropractor, massage therapist, and naturopathic doctor.

Frequently Asked Questions

Following are the questions that our patients tend to ask and our methods of answering them.

Question #1: What is neurofeedback?

Answer: Neurofeedback training (NFT) is a brain-based method of treatment that retrains the brain to function and regulate in a more effective way. It literally teaches the brain to be more adaptive, efficient, and effective. Many individuals seeking help for depression, anxiety, concentration, sleep, and addiction issues find tremendous and permanent relief.

Through EEG brainwave recordings and audio/visual signals, the NF machine monitors the brainwaves and re-trains them through auditory and visual stimulation. The result is a more efficient, optimally performing brain state.

We use an ultra-low-frequency training technique. The brain learns how to better self-regulate its thoughts, feelings, and arousal levels. NFT works as if the computer screen is a mirror for the brain; it magnifies areas that are not working as efficiently as they could, and it trains the brain to operate more effectively.

We have also acquired another system that is used specifically for concussions and TBIs. This is similar to the LENS system, which uses a tiny microcurrent that is fed to the brain. The brain takes what it needs to regulate itself. This system is very effective for brain injuries.

Question #2: Are there any risks? What about permanent brain damage?

Answer: With regard to risk or harm, there is no evidence either from our practitioners' experiences with clients, the clients, or the literature that the treatment is harmful or that it creates or has negative side effects. NFT is completely non-invasive and painless. Some clients have reported that training seemed to cause temporary feelings of drowsiness or fatigue, as well as occasional headaches. These symptoms were not serious and usually resolve on their own within twelve to twenty-four hours, or they can be corrected by shifting the brainwave target range and electrode locations.

Typically, these problems resolve quickly. Therefore, it's very important that you keep your neurotherapist informed of any changes or negative effects, even if they seem unconnected to neurofeedback, so that the training can be modified.

Question #3: What does neurofeedback help?

Answer: NFT has been used for a variety of conditions that appear to be associated with irregular brainwave activity, including attention deficit disorder (ADD) with and without hyperactivity (ADHD), as well as specific learning disabilities. NFT has also shown promise with certain behavioral disorders (eating disorders, addictions, and OCD), sleep problems, depression, migraine, anxiety, chronic pain, minor head injury, and seizure disorders.

Our clinical evaluation will determine an individualized treatment protocol for your brain based on the questions you answered in your initial evaluation with a trained practitioner.

Typically, there are three types of training you may receive: Beta, SMR, and/or Alpha/Theta. In general, beta training is provided for clients who have under-arousal of the left or right hemispheres, which disrupts one's ability to focus and concentrate. SMR, which is a training of the beta wave at a different frequency, supports calming, relaxation, and objectivity.

A combination of Beta and SMR creates overall stability of brainwave activity and is particularly helpful for individuals with long-term mental health issues, chronic substance use disorders, head injuries, and a history of mental illness in their family of origin. Alpha/Theta training, frequently utilized for clients with PTSD, traumatic histories, and Axis

II Cluster B disorders, creates a distinct feeling of peace and serenity, emotional connection to others, and more objective observational skills, all frequently lacking in traumatized individuals here (Shari Stillman-Corbitt, Psy.D., 2010).

The following summary, cited from Dr. Corbitt (2010), further explains the purposes and uses for the different protocols:

- **Beta/SMR protocols help:** Better focus and concentration, more present, improves objectivity, mood further stabilizes, more calm and relaxed.

- **Alpha/Theta protocols help:** Less self-absorbed, more open-minded, less defended, more connected emotionally, increased peace and serenity, have more objective observations, and access and integrate repressed experiences.

We assess for developmental trauma and then determine what type of training we will conduct based on the findings of the clinical interview.

Question #4: How long will it take?

Answer: Every brain responds to NFT differently. Someone with multiple target issues may necessitate a longer treatment. For mild to moderate symptoms, a person can expect to have anywhere from twenty to forty sessions. For moderate to severe symptoms, the number of sessions can reach sixty or more. The growth areas that are targeted in NFT are monitored and rated each week to determine improvement.

Many times a person will feel a change in their bodies, arousal state, and sleep patterns after a few sessions, but in order to successfully resolve symptoms, a consistent treatment plan, consisting of *at least* two or three sessions per week, is needed.

Question #5: How long do the results last?

Answer: The end goal of NFT is always to *resolve* each identified symptom. While each client and protocol is different, requiring different lengths of treatment, the effects of NFT are proven to be lasting and stable (see the Appendix). With NFT, the brain reorganizes itself by forming new neural pathways or activating unused ones as it expands functionality, as do all the abilities we develop, so that the gains made with NFT are typically permanent.

Question #6: How long has NFT been around?

Answer: Many neuroscientists dating back to the 1950s have utilized brain biofeedback and brain training. Over the years, scientists have studied and streamlined their understanding of brain training using EEG machines, fMRIs (functional magnetic resonance imaging), and brain mapping. For the past ten to fifteen years, only highly trained neurologists and neuropsychologists have been able to perform neurofeedback brain training due to the high sensitivity and complexity of the machines available to them at that time.

In recent years, more user-friendly machines and programs have been developed and are on the market for psychotherapists, physicians, and trained neurofeedback practitioners to use. The system we have is one used by many Olympic athletes for peak performance. This low-frequency system also has more games that children enjoy playing!

Please see our list of research articles and recommended readings for a more thorough history of neurofeedback.

Question #7: Is there any scientific or empirical research to back NFT up?

Answer: There is *tons* of scientific and empirical research to support the efficacy of neurofeedback brain training. There are over 1,200 empirical studies that have been conducted on the efficacy of neurofeedback. The website isnr.org has a listing of all the studies, including the most recent ones.

Question #8: How much does it cost?

Answer: The prices for neurofeedback range from $150 to $250 per session, depending on the experience of the treating provider.

Question #9: Does it hurt?

Answer: No, NFT is a completely pain-free and noninvasive treatment modality. As we noted previously, the most common side effects typically tend to be drowsiness or fatigue. Some people report a slight headache directly after the session, but these reports are not typical and usually resolve by the next morning.

Question #10: What does a typical session look like?

Answer: During your initial evaluation, your practitioner will evaluate your goals and symptoms in depth. If the client is a minor, the parents will be asked to participate in the initial evaluation. If the client is a younger child (under the age of 13), it is not necessary for the child to be present for the initial evaluation, as the parent will be a better judge of their own child's symptoms and target growth areas.

Initial evaluations can occur either in the office or over the phone. We recommend that if the client is a small child, the initial evaluation be performed over the phone prior to coming into the office.

During the first session, you will sit in a comfortable chair while the practitioner places sensors on your scalp using a conductive paste—its consistency is similar to a very soft wax—or a wet sponge. Absolutely *nothing* is inserted inside of your body or scalp.

Next, you will sit back and watch a spaceship flying through a tunnel. There is music with the system as well as a teddy bear that is buzzing on your lap. During the entire session, your brain is doing all of the work without your conscious effort—it is truly brain training! You can also watch a movie and be in the session.

The feedback is that the screen becomes small when your brain is not doing what we want it to do. Therefore your brain does the work to increase the size of the movie screen so you can see the actual movie. The brain is receiving the exercise as it does the work. Each session is typically 45 minutes to one hour, and you are free to return to work, drive, or complete your day after leaving the session.

Question #11: What if I am taking medications? Will that interfere with NFT?

Answer: The only class of medication that interferes with the effectiveness of NFT are benzodiazepines (Xanax, Klonopin,

Valium) and only if taken in very high dosages on a daily basis.

Question #12: Does insurance cover neurofeedback?

Answer: Some insurance companies may cover neurofeedback. However, it doesn't hurt to explore the possibility of coverage. The insurance company may reference this as a CPT code 90901 (biofeedback by any modality) and 90876. If your insurance company will authorize training, you will typically pay for services up front and apply for reimbursement.

Questions to Ask Your Health Insurance Company:

1. Does my policy cover EEG biofeedback (Code 90876) for my diagnosis of _____ and/or _____? (Be sure to consult Healthy Within or your referring provider for your diagnosis.)

2. What percentage is reimbursed, since Healthy Within is an out-of-network provider?

3. Do I need a prescription or letter from my MD to say that it is medically necessary?

4. How many sessions of biofeedback will you cover? Per week? Per year?

5. Is there a limit of the total amount paid out? (for example, capping out at $1,500 each year)

6. Because Healthy Within is an out-of-network provider, do I need to see my primary care physician to make a referral to them?

Question #13: What about a placebo effect?

Answer: There is absolutely no placebo effect with neu-rofeedback. Placebos do not work on animals, and that is how this field was discovered. Don't worry, as with humans, no animals were harmed. As a matter of fact, the cats came running for their session when they saw the researcher arrive.

Research Studies with Neurofeedback

The neurofeedback research community is buzzing with excitement. We have increasing numbers of neuroscientists who are incredibly intrigued by the successes they experience with neurofeedback regulation. It is apparent that this will be the decade of decoding the brain.

Grants and increased funding are being made available for us to study the brain more. The increased attention that has emerged from the mindfulness community has enhanced the importance of paying attention to the brain and the mind.

One just has to look up books on Amazon on the brain, and you'll see that thousands of new titles show up. When the Dalai Lama invited neuroscientists to join him in Dharamsala, India, and extended an open invitation to merge their science into the science of the mind, he opened the floodgates of exploration.

It is only a matter of time before major neuroscientists like Richard Davidson, Dan Siegel, and Rick Hanson begin to mention neurofeedback on a consistent basis. Bessel Van der Kolk, a leader in the area of PTSD, has conducted a double-blind study showcasing the effectiveness of neuro-feedback for PTSD. Currently, some of the neuroscientists are still enamored with the fMRI machines, which are giving us neurofeedback practitioners a wealth of information about where we can pinpoint our treatment targets.

One of the best websites that offers the most up-to-date research from all over the world is the EEGInfo website (www.eeginfo.com). Siegfried Othmer, one of the founders of EEGInfo, is a lead scientist and a physicist, indicating his varied and extensive interests. This website has the majority of the research articles in the field of neurotherapy.

Our national certification organizations also offer re-search articles that are easy to locate and read. There are over 1,200 published articles in neurofeedback. Two of these organizations are ISNR (International Society for Neuro-feedback and Research) and BCIA (Biofeedback Certification International Alliance).

D. Corydon Hammond has created a comprehensive, 37-page neurofeedback research guide, which offers a clear idea of the massive amount of research that is available on neu-rofeedback. This bibliography can be found on the ISNR website (isnr.org), and each topic area is clearly highlighted.

There are multiple studies that address every area of treatment for neurofeedback. As a result, once clinicians dis-cover neurofeedback, they become consumed by the amount of progress they can see in their clients. The average length of time in which one begins to see progress is within 12 to 20 sessions. The majority of patients will continue on, since they see benefits in numerous areas of functioning.

For example, they may have come in for insomnia, which begins to get resolved. However, they see benefits in multiple areas such as better energy, clearer focus, less emotional reactivity, and a general feeling of well being.

At our treatment center, we consistently receive referrals from psychiatrists, neurologists, pediatricians, naturopathic doctors, speech pathologists, coaches, orthopedic doctors, autism specialists, endocrinologists, pain management specialists and, of course, psychologists and psychotherapists in our community.

CHAPTER 3

CONDITIONS THAT NEUROFEEDBACK HELPS

"The literature, which lacks any negative study of substance, suggests that EEG Biofeedback (Neurofeedback) therapy should play a major therapeutic role in many different areas. In my opinion, if any medication had demonstrated such a wide spectrum of efficacy, it would be universally accepted and widely used."

~ Frank Duffy, M.D., Head Neurologist, Harvard Medical School

AS WE HAVE SEEN from the previous chapter, the brain is the Grand Central Station of our entire body. It is apparent that if one of the main train tracks leading into New York City broke down, there would be massive congestion that would immobilize thousands of New Yorkers.

The brain is an incredibly self-regulatory system that, if given the right conditions, can optimize itself. The main driving force of the brain is via electrical impulses. When these electrical impulses are dysregulated, it dysregulates the entire brain which, in turn, dysregulates the whole body.

Neurofeedback as a treatment modality is becoming increasingly recognized as a powerful brain training method that is able to arrest numerous dysregulated brain states. Through neurofeedback, brain health is restored, increasing the quality of life for numerous people who had settled into a semi-functional way of living.

My years of clinical experience were in the field of depression, OCD, anxiety, alcoholism, PTSD, and eating disorders. Healthy Within's hallmark as a cutting-edge center in NFT is as a multidisciplinary, integrative treatment center. So, integrating neurofeedback as one of our primary treatment modalities was a natural evolution of our years of experience with various brain states and the different early treatment methods in this area.

The goal of neurofeedback is to cultivate optimum brain conditions that helps balance a person's life. The essence of neuroplasticity gives us hope that the brain is not a static, "frozen" organ. Neuroplasticity refers to the ability of the brain to grow new neurons at any stage in a person's life.

Neuronal regeneration means that even when we have poor neuronal activity, with neurofeedback, we are able to give the brain a new lease on life. The brain is being recharged and new cells are forming and new pathways are being created. The brain does not have to die a slow death.

The following are conditions that are able to be impacted with much success via neurofeedback:

- ADD/ADHD
- addictions (alcohol, drugs, pornography, Internet, gaming, sex, gambling)
- anxiety
- Asperger's/autism spectrum
- chemo brain
- chronic pain
- depression
- dyslexia/other learning disorders
- fibromyalgia
- improving athletic, musical, singing performance

- insomnia
- migraines/headaches
- OCD (obsessive compulsive disorder)
- PTSD (post-traumatic stress disorder)
- stroke
- stuttering
- Tourette's syndrome/tics
- traumatic brain injury (TBI)
- trichotillomania

In the next section, we'll give a brief overview of the conditions that can be treated by neurofeedback as they relate to adult brains and teen and children's brains.

Teen Brains

Neuroscience is shedding a ton of light on the "wild" side of the teen brain. Teens are acutely susceptible to stress, peer pressure, and other negative forces due to their underdeveloped prefrontal cortex. Remember, the teen brain is still under construction. During these years, dopamine rushes are the highest and most profound in the teen brain.

So, risky behavior among teens can often be the hallmark that parents fear the most, since the "let me think about it" part of the brain has not grown at all yet. The "sure, that sounds awesome" part of the brain can dominate. Novelty is what the teen brain craves and longs for. The imbalance between amygdala and frontal lobe control in their brains may explain their minor and major at-risk behaviors, from arguing over a homework assignment to drug experimentation and unprotected sex (Feinstein, 2009).

A unique biological event occurs in the brains of boys because of the increase in testosterone. This rapid increase in testosterone makes the amygdala grow bigger. When compared to girl's brains, the amygdala in boys is significantly larger. This larger amygdala explains why the aggressiveness and at-risk behavior in boys is greater than in girls. Not all boys, of course, will act aggressively since their temperament and what parents and teachers expose them to makes a huge impact.

It is this risk-taking brain that is very prone to developing addictions to alcohol, cutting, drugs, the Internet, video gaming, texting, and pornography. Neurofeedback is able to nudge the brain away from the stress so that the craving for the fix subsides.

At our center, we have worked with hundreds of teens whose stress factors have triggered addictions. With a combined approach of training the brain for activation of the prefrontal cortex and empathetic validation of their feelings, the success has been highly rewarding.

It's important to note that we may have a teen who comes in for one issue, and the whole teen brain regulation creates balance in multiple other areas of their life. Neurofeedback reorganizes the entire brain.

Teens and Children Treated with Neurofeedback

The brains of teens and young adults are still very much under construction. When the railroad tracks are being laid for trains to travel on, the engineers and construction workers are very careful to level out the land properly, making sure that there is stability and consistency so that the train has a smooth ride. Carelessness on the part of the engineers could result in fatal train wrecks.

Neurofeedback can be seen as a methodology that makes the brain's electrical impulses more efficient, particularly when the brain is in its "pruning" phase, so that, similar to the smooth train ride, the brain "fires" and performs smoothly.

"Use it or lose it" is a phrase that applies very appropriately to teen brains. When a child is born, the brain mass consists of the brain stem, limbic brain, and neocortex. The child's brain can be seen as a structure where the frame has been established and none of the wiring, structures, or walls have been formed.

The range of experiences that children and teens have will determine the health of the brain. In other words, the entire life cycle of the life of the brain is determined by what the brain experiences in its early formative years, particularly the teen years.

Some common conditions treated by neurofeedback among children and teens are dyslexia, ADHD, OCD, trichotillomania, headaches, migraines, and anxiety. There are some sociocultural perspectives that put the teen brain at risk.

The brains of our youth are in a state of rapid adaptation and change considering the technological revolution that we are in. In the last ten years, children and teens have become exposed to more media than the majority of adults have been exposed to in their lifetimes. The excessive excitation of the neuronal circuitry in the brain is creating children whose attention spans are equal to the seven to twelve minutes of a TV show before a commercial interruption.

In 2015, I presented at a local high school in San Diego. My topic was "Sex, Drugs, Rock & Roll, and the Teen Brain." Needless to say, as the teens entered the room, their dopamine circuits lit up when they saw the word "sex." Each class had between fifty to seventy ninth- and tenth-grade boys and girls. I had been given the onerous task of keeping them engaged and learning for ninety minutes. It had been about two years since I had been in front of large class sizes like these. I was scheduled to teach three ninety-minute classes each day, a total of six classes of fifty to seventy kids in each class.

I knew that I was going to be deeply challenged in keeping their attention focused on my favorite subject: the teen brain! Fortunately, at the time I had a fifteen-year-old at home, which means that we have the real-time knowledge of our son's experience.

As I prepared for this wonderful and challenging task, I knew that my teaching style would have to mirror the smartphone generation's attention span. I was determined to make my presentation engaging, fun, and interactive.

Having the knowledge that the teen brain has the engine of a Ferrari and the brakes of a go-cart, spending ninety minutes in front of dozens of teens would require my neuroscience background. Of course, I wanted to hear the advice of the brain we have at home.

The wisest words my son gave me were, "Mom, make sure you don't talk for longer than nine to eleven minutes, then put on a YouTube video. Get them to tell you what they thought—make sure you let them talk. They will connect with you if you hear them!"

Does he sound like the child of a psychologist? I chose bright video clips that were no longer than three to four minutes, and I put some pieces of edgy language in the presentation. I was making sure that these amygdala-driven brains were firing short growth spurts of dopamine.

In the middle of the presentation, I included a short clip of "Your Brain on Porn." The response from the fourteen- and fifteen-year-olds was amazing. This particular clip allowed them to see how their brains are anatomically affected by pornography.

During these years, teens feel everything very intensely. Memories that are formed in our teen years remain as vivid as ever because adolescence is the time when our brain receives the most amount of dopamine. First, let's examine the social construct of adolescence.

Prior to the Great Depression here in the United States, there was no such thing as adolescence. The majority of Americans didn't even graduate from high school. Once kids reached their teen years, they farmed, helped the family businesses, and worked in factories and stores. These "teens" spent all their time with adults and so, their peer culture became the adult culture. Today, teens spend sixty hours a week with their cohorts and sixteen hours a week with their parents.

With social media, now teens spend less than one hour a day interacting with their parents. High schools have become the vehicle through which mass dysregulation of the amygdala takes place.

High schools create their own peculiar culture with norms that are not necessarily ones that enhance the prefrontal cortex. Risky behavior is condoned, and doing wild and crazy things makes one very popular. In the teen world, it's even better if you are able to get away with it!

In summary, in the 1940s we didn't have adolescence, and we didn't have nearly the numbers of teen depression, suicide, cutting, anxiety, and eating disorders that we have now. A high school is an arena fraught with difficulties on how to find one's self and create an identity.

High schools are huge institutions that create a pecking order of sorts for one to define themselves. Many of us adults have heard high school students making statements about how they want to be different from their peers, yet doing exactly what their peers are doing.

From a brain science perspective, since these years from fourteen to twenty-three are the years when the neurons are doing the most amount of pruning, what this brain is exposed to is what this brain will be guided toward for the rest of its life.

When teens' and children's brains are overstimulated and not given the right food and rest, we inadvertently put the growing brain at risk. Lack of sleep in the teen years is the highest risk factor for the development of depression. Think of how many numbers of teens get by with less than six hours of sleep per night because they are overscheduled with their activities. These risks then create conditions that are becoming the norm of our language in the 21st century: depression, anxiety, eating disorders, cutting, drug addictions, and so on.

Neurofeedback is a powerful treatment of choice for many of these dysregulated brain states because we have seen antidepressants creating severe complications among children and teens. We have treated countless teens whose anxiety and depression worsened after they were put on medications like Prozac, Zoloft, Effexor, Paxil, and Cymbalta.

As a cognitive neuroscientist who is also a seasoned psychologist, my almost three decades of treating children and particularly teens has enabled me to prescribe what may be the best combined therapy for these teens.

One of the conditions commonly treated by neurofeedback is separation anxiety among children. We find that anxiety tends to run in families, and it can often begin to manifest itself in a variety of ways. Anxious children fear unpredictability. The beginning of school can be a very scary time for anxious, sensitive children. Separation anxiety can often be a predictor of different types of anxiety to emerge in later years.

Anxiety can manifest as hair pulling (trichotillomania) and OCD (obsessive compulsive disorder). Most people are not aware of OCD as an anxiety disorder; basically, the anxious mind is worrying. Some children and teens that develop OCD often have fears, worries, and dread of the night coming on. Their brain begins to throw off tons of cortisol and epinephrine. The amygdala in the brain is aroused, and the body goes into fight-or-flight mode. Our brains are programmed to sense danger. The brains of highly sensitive, anxious children and teens are acutely aware of their surroundings.

The majority of parents are not aware that separation anxiety in early childhood will lead to more anxious states, particularly as the child goes through puberty. Neurofeedback can regulate that anxious brain at the early stages so that we are not dealing with severe OCD at age nine or ten. Fears and phobias are two conditions that are most responsive to neurofeedback. The neural circuitry of the amygdala is very responsive to the "nudging" the brain receives. Typically there would be excitatory impulses, likely high beta waves. The exposure to the different brainwave frequency calms the brain down. The fear loop is broken and the brain loop begins to recover from the trauma.

The brains of teens are particularly responsive to neurofeedback because the myelin sheath of the brain is still being formed. In other words, the foundation is being established for this super highway, and the small nudges received from neurofeedback can have monumental, long-lasting effects.

The current subculture of adolescence is a particularly stressful time for our teens. Depression and suicide rates among teens are the highest in this past decade. Conservative estimates state that about 21% of teens and children experience depression and anxiety. Pressures from academic achievement, juggling sports, and the demands of the peer culture all put teens at risk for depression. Certainly one must look at the genetics within the family. Our experience has been that depression and anxiety will often exist together.

Our treatment protocols are very holistic in nature. Because we look at the whole person, our evaluation for every teen is going to encompass the entire biopsychosocial perspective. The evaluation process is very thorough as we examine all aspects of the teen's life including food, nutrition, sleep routines, hobbies, interests, exercise, social circles, Internet usage, and how many technology devices they have, including time spent on each.

Evaluation of resiliency is additionally a critical part of this evaluation. Many teens cultivate incredible creative outlets; to accurately know their strengths, we want to see where they blossom.

ADHD

Attention deficit disorder, both the hyperactive and inattentive types, responds extremely well to neurofeedback. Dr. Leonard Sax, a prominent pediatrician who also has a Ph.D., clearly points to the overmedication of our children with ADHD meds, particularly boys.

There is a tremendous drive in many communities to pathologize the normally active, curious, reaching self of the child. As our industrialization of food has created numerous autoimmune conditions, children's brains with respect to attention and focus are clearly impacted. Massive amounts of preservatives and color additives have been clearly pinpointed and seem to correlate with the rise in ADHD/ADD diagnoses for children and teens.

Some startling CDC statistics indicate that as of 2007, 5.4 million children in the United States were diagnosed with ADHD. The percentage of children with parent-reported ADHD increased by 22% from 2003 to 2007. Even more startling is that rates of ADHD diagnosis increased an average of 3% per year from 1997 to 2006 and an average of 5.5% from 2003 to 2007. This was about eight years ago; imagine what the updated increase might be!

Slow brainwave activity (theta waves) is at the core of ADHD. Medications temporarily speed up the brain but once the medications are removed, the brainwaves slow down again. Neurofeedback helps train the brain waves so that they speed up to an optimum place and communicate better with other brain regions. Once these waves are in a good, solid range and the brain is happy, it works to sustain itself in that calm, focused place.

The American Academy of Pediatrics clearly recommends neurofeedback as the first treatment of choice for ADHD/ADD. Since we are treating the whole brain, children with ADD not only improve their concentration, focus, and ability to sit still and complete tasks, but their personalities become happier.

Additionally, our experience has been that these kids start to have more friends. The brain is designed to function in an optimum way. Neurofeedback restores that optimum functioning to the brain. Our brains are designed to be focused, creative, reasonable, and efficient.

The statistics also show that some of the highest prescription of ADHD meds is in low-income, ethnically diverse communities. The poverty in these areas and lack of knowledge of proper nutrition make a huge difference. If we had free neurofeedback clinics in the projects and in some of the lowest-income areas, there is an absolute guarantee that our jails would get emptied.

Advocates of young Latino and African-American youth all speak of the way in which there is a pipeline from the public schools to the jails, with ADD/ADHD being the "label" these so-called "bad kids" are given. It would be no surprise that the main opponents of neurofeedback are the huge pharmaceutical companies that have billions of dollars at their disposal to woo the psychiatrists and the physicians.

One of the most interesting successes with the treatment of *any* condition with neurofeedback is that even as we may be targeting oppositional behavior, temper tantrums, tics, or sullen moods, there is an improvement in numerous other areas of the child's life.

At our center, we may have a child who comes in for teeth grinding, or bruxism. As we target neurofeedback for the bruxism, it doesn't surprise us any more when Mom continues to comment about how pleasant Johnny has become, and how he is happier, sleeping better, and is significantly more focused on his schoolwork.

Parents who have children or teens that are athletes are continually amazed at the way in which their teen suddenly started to improve with their tennis or golf games.

Dyslexia

Dyslexia is another learning condition that has seen tremendous success from neurofeedback. Dr. Clare Albright uses a very powerful analogy when she notes that the brain of a child with learning disabilities is like a truck that is stuck in low gear, and the driver has forgotten that higher gears even exist. The frustration that is felt can be so disheartening that many people with dyslexia give up trying and settle for a slow, grinding, and bumpy ride through life.

Neurofeedback as a tool then says to the brain, "Look, here are some other gears you can use." The other gears are the various other brainwave frequencies that lie undiscovered in the brain's potential. In a 1985 study, the researchers were shocked to discover that the IQ points of their subjects increased by 15 points. This can be attributed to the wiring in the brain being more efficient, hence memory would be improved and retention of material would be more solid. When the various regions of the brain are talking to each other more efficiently, it makes sense that the scoring on various measures of IQ tests would improve dramatically.

Autism Spectrum Disorders/Asperger's Syndrome

Autism spectrum conditions, including Asperger's Syndrome (which is no longer in the DSM-5), have been very successfully treated by neurofeedback. The incidence of autism increased dramatically in the 1990s. As with ADHD, the high levels of autism can vary greatly, with very mild conditions (Asperger's) hardly impacting a person's functioning.

Many high-functioning people with Asperger's (Aspies) are some of the most creative individuals in our last two centuries. It is common knowledge that Bill Gates, Mark Zuckerberg, and Albert Einstein all have (or had) Asperger's. Many autistic brains present neuronal dysregulation in that it is difficult for these kids to soothe themselves, unable to synthesize emotions, and show repetitive behaviors.

When a comprehensive QEEG (quantitative electroencephalography) is conducted on a child with autism, each person will have specific brain regions that are affected. Patterns that frequently emerge arc deficiencies in slow-wave amplitudes in the back of the brain and excessive slow frequency in the frontal area of the brain, but mostly in the right frontal cortex. Frequently, we will see dysfunction in the ACG (anterior cingulate gyrus). The deficiency of theta waves in the back of the brain is associated with poor stress tolerance, edginess, sleep disturbances, and a general inability to calm down.

Our ability to see ourselves as separate, emotional human beings resides in the right frontal cortex. The ACC is the part of the brain that regulates thoughts, emotions, and motor behaviors. Among many high-functioning autistic children, if the activity of the ACC is very high, that would cause the OCD behavior we see in many autistic and Asperger's children.

There have been a number of excellent studies on the effectiveness of neurofeedback with autism. One study by Dr. Robert Coben in 2007 with thirty-seven patients done on Asperger's children showed an 89% improvement. He had created three phases of treatment, and the overall improvement with all the children was an average of 80%. The frontal disconnectivity in the brain was treated with neurofeedback where the focus was increased inter-hemispheric connectivity. This type of frontal inter-hemispheric training is what created the successful results.

In summary, children's and teen's brains are highly receptive to the influences of brainwave training via neurofeedback. Similar results have been experienced with adults and neurofeedback. In the next section, we'll explore the large numbers of conditions that neurofeedback is able to treat with adults.

Neurofeedback and Adults

Within the category of mood conditions, neurofeedback successfully treats depression, anxiety, OCD, eating disorders, alcoholism, substance abuse, and insomnia. Our experience and the experience of other neurotherapists is that when we begin to treat anxiety, the mood lifts. If we are treating the classic symptoms of OCD, then anxiety lifts. Each of these conditions tends to have sleep dysregulation as a part of their medical condition that the patients are struggling with.

Adult brains are highly responsive to neurofeedback. For most adults, by the time they are exploring alternative treatments for their depression, anxiety, or ADD, they have lost years in trying to find solutions, thereby feeling incredibly discouraged. Some of the most successful outcomes with neurofeedback are with depression, anxiety, OCD, and panic/phobia disorders.

An area of study that has received its first research-based study is looking at the effectiveness of neurofeedback with cognitive impairments that emerge after chemotherapy. This condition is popularly referred to as "chemo brain." Chemotherapy agents are powerful cell killers that kill healthy cells along with cancer cells. Regions of the brain that are often affected will present issues of sleep, memory, digestion, lack of memory, and loss of pleasure in activities.

This study, conducted at the Cleveland Clinic in Ohio, showed that after ten sessions, the brain recalibrates itself to what it was prior to chemotherapy. Of the twenty-three women who participated in the study, twenty-one reported returning to normal levels of functioning. The lingering cognitive effects from chemotherapy can last for as long as twenty years after treatment. Neurofeedback has helped many women achieve optimum brain fitness after as few as twenty sessions.

Similarly, we have found identical results with PMS symptoms, which we tend to classify more in the pain region treatment modalities with neurofeedback. PMS, PMDD (premenstrual dysphoric disorder), fibromyalgia, arthritis, and migraines are all adult conditions that neurofeedback treats very successfully. Because the symptoms of PMS have a lot in common with depression, many doctors will place patients on small doses of antidepressant medications for PMS.

Clearly, the whole brain and body are in an imbalance when a person is experiencing PMS. The hormones and neurotransmitter changes coursing through the body are clearly coming from a highly "inflamed" brain. As the CEO of the body, the brain can exert control over numerous regions within itself and bring it to harmony.

Signals of pain travel via a neural network in the brain; so, if the neural networks are rerouted to make them more efficient in the transmission of nerve impulses, one would see the benefit that neurofeedback would have with pain modulation.

Standard medical treatment would consist of medications that block the pain. These medications mask the symptoms of pain, with the underlying "ghost pain" still being very present in the brain. This is the reason why patients need increased dosages of medication to cope with the pain.

Neurofeedback teaches a person to control their internal physical responses using an EEG and a biofeedback machine. As the individual observes their own brain doing the work to reduce the pain, they feel more in control and know where to take their brain if they experience the pain. With the neurofeedback machine, they have figured out which brainwave pattern is best for them to beat.

Many people who experience chronic pain have had histories of trauma in their lives. Approximately 85% of people with chronic pain have experienced some type of emotional, physical, or psychological trauma. People who have chronic pain may have underarousal in their brains. For people with chronic pain conditions, it's important for them to be in psychotherapy as well because sometimes the trauma memories can reemerge with neurofeedback.

Our protocols at our treatment center tend to be very holistic and comprehensive. We incorporate a variety of therapeutic techniques including acupuncture, Alpha-Stim, massage, craniosacral therapy, naturopathy, as well as neuro-therapy.

Migraine and headache sufferers have experienced significant relief from neurofeedback treatments. In fact, when people with migraines come to us for neurofeedback, we prepare them to be startled that their headaches will subside and almost disappear.

Forty-five million people in the United States suffer from headaches. We know that women who have delivered babies using epidural injections for pain are often left with chronic headaches. How many of these women were informed that they might have the side effect of a headache that will last a lifetime?

The drugstores in our communities are loaded with tons of choices for pain management with over-the-counter medications. Clinical reports from seasoned neurotherapists who have been treating migraines and headaches for over twenty years state that eight out of ten of their patients no longer have migraines!

Within the Asperger's/Autism Spectrum Disorder with adults, neurofeedback has been just as effective. Enhanced awareness of the environment, coupled with dialing into the needs of others, can begin to create more happiness in the families who have adult ASD people.

At our center, one extra piece that we add with our patients with ASD is the prescription of oxytocin. UCSD researcher Dr. Jaime Pineda has conducted extensive studies on the positive impact of oxytocin on the brains of people who lean toward autism. This is commonly known in popular culture as the "love drug," since this is the hormone that flows through our bodies when we bond, attach, have empathy, and are in love!

Of course, behavioral therapies such as social skills training and psychotherapy are an integral part of the multidimensional treatment plan. Typically, their family practice doctor or a naturopath prescribes the oxytocin.

The cultivation of empathy is a very important part of a goal, and training the right prefrontal region is an important goal of neurotherapy. We see our patients becoming more aware and attuned with their loved ones. We are actually able to see the actions of the mirror neurons. Three months prior to that, the patient would not have even noticed a beautiful child or an adorable dog. The results feel very encouraging to the family members who see them *oohing* and *aahing* over cute animals or children.

Athletes

An exciting area of work with neurofeedback has been with those of us who work with athletes. I'll cover this area in depth in Chapter 5. Soccer teams, tennis players, golfers, and other athletes commonly utilize neurofeedback as a tool for "brain focus." It allows them to practice being in the "zone" with much more intensity, thereby increasing their chances of faster reaction times and the immediate burst of energy they need their body to produce.

The essence of training is learning the links between our physical behavior or internal attitudes and the quality of brain functioning through the use of parameters that are created by the brain frequencies that we desire. There is an intentional managing of mind operation for a set of desired results that is the hallmark of athletics.

The purpose of peak performance is the greater usage of the potential of one's mind in order to act more effectively, to obtain better achievements, and, of course, to lead a more joyful and successful life. The benefits include better concentration, focus, and attention, as well as earlier decision-making, shorter response time, more efficient memory, accelerated learning, reduced number of errors, quicker and deeper relaxation, reduced anxiety, and reduced stage fright. What athlete is going to say no to any of the above?

Neurofeedback for Veterans/Military

Perhaps the two areas that have been the most exciting in conditions we treat are PTSD and TBI. We have so many wounded soldiers that are returning from almost two decades of war. These young brains have not only been traumatized by the violence, but they have also experienced physical trauma to the brain as a result of explosives going off around them.

The VA, military, and naval hospitals are all incorporating neurofeedback as one of the treatments for PTSD and TBI. The brains of these soldiers are healing well. Numerous studies are underway to add to the existing knowledge that neurofeedback works for any kind of trauma to the brain. Because the brain is hard-wired for a certain type of electrical activity, the disruption experienced by a head injury or trauma can be extremely destabilizing for the brain.

We have seen studies showing the efficacy of neurofeedback with trauma since the late 1980s. Flashbacks with

PTSD seem to resolve fairly quickly with the introduction of the Alpha/Theta protocol. Many patients with PTSD will report not having slept through the night in years. In some of our own recent patients, often eight to twelve sessions of neurofeedback resolve the flashbacks, which do not return!

When a person's fight–flight mechanism has been triggered so intensely as in the case of being in any kind of war zone, domestic violence in the home, or the wars in the Middle East, the heightened cortical arousal of the brain is the target of neurofeedback. Alpha/Theta protocol asks the individual to recall one event that has caused distress. After that heightened arousal, we introduce Alpha/Theta training, in which we want to evoke the calming alpha waves to override the agitated high beta waves that show up.

The results of controlled studies, as well as clinical experience, have been very encouraging. People who have been suffering for many years with an over-aroused brain finally begin to get the rest they so deserve. Follow-up testing with many people has shown that their gains are maintained. Release from the trauma opens up so much more psychic energy for the person to begin to cultivate other areas in their life.

Tics, Tourette's, the aging brain, and strokes are also common conditions in adults treated by neurofeedback. Because a stroke is seen as an injury to the brain, the same treatment we use for traumatic brain injury is what we would use for strokes.

Speech therapists are shocked at the progress they see with their patients if concomitant neurotherapy is also taking place. Movement disorders respond favorably, as we are able to localize the region of damage and then conduct neurotherapy in the sites that need activation.

The emergent clarity we have regarding neuroplasticity and regeneration of damaged neurons and dendrites has been one of the most exciting descriptions of what neurotherapy does in the brain.

Functional brain imaging is showing neuroscientists the very specific localized areas that are impaired in the brain. So, we expect that neurotherapists will soon begin to start conducting fMRI-guided neurofeedback. This has already begun in some centers. Currently, when we conduct the QEEG, it gives us highly specific targeted information on the regions of the brain that need more activation and the areas that need less activation. Through the symptom inventories we conduct in neurotherapy, we are able to be highly accurate in identifying which areas of the brain need activation or inhibition.

The future for neurofeedback is exciting. This chapter is intended to provide hope in the wide range of conditions that can be treated by neurofeedback.

CHAPTER 4

WHAT MAKES A BRAIN THRIVE?

*To raise new questions, new possibilities, to regard old
problems from a new angle, requires creative
imagination and marks real advance in science.*

~ Albert Einstein

HAPPY, SUCCESSFUL PEOPLE seem to love certain ways of being in the world where they seem to maximize their opportunities and appear to have a friendly relationship with failure. They seem to know how to be in the "zone," as well as be productive and relaxed at the same time. These power-packed, winning, supercharged brains are worthwhile to understand.

While much of what this book appears to be discussing is the brain, we can't ignore the fact that the mind is the seat of consciousness. Obviously, what the mind wishes and the brain computes may live in opposition with each other.

This resilient, supercharged winner's brain is a product of its genetics and the environment it is bathed in. These brains operate quite differently than the average brain. They are very good at tuning out distractions and choosing the best way to focus on a task in order to get the best outcome. These brains can somehow create a channel of harnessing extra focusing power to help them perform better, despite interruptions.

Another feature these brains seem to have is that they have a bottomless effort supply. They seem to know how to become motivated and can push through boredom. Being able to push through unpleasant, boring tasks and persisting makes this power-packed brain highly adaptable, contributing to its neuroplasticity. The ability to pay attention, remain present, and gravitate toward new, inspiring things is another way this thriving brain works.

The Dalai Lama stated, "In a real sense the brain we develop reflects the life we lead." The brain we are born with is the raw material we have been given, and what we do with this raw material cultivates a supercharged, Zen brain. There are thousands of ways in which we can shape our brain to more fully express its potential.

Neurogenesis (the growth of neurons) exists even in the 90-year-old brain! Because the brain never stops growing, we can start a Ph.D. at age 80 or even 85, thereby giving the brain one of the things it cherishes the most—stimulation. There are countless ways in which an infant, child, teenager, and adult's brain can be stimulated.

Traits of a Well Brain

As we admire people around us who seem to have equanimity, poise, a sense of calm, focus, and happiness, we wonder how they seem to be able to create that wholesomeness.

The mind plays a profoundly powerful role in the cultivation of a healthy brain. The well brain being described here is a combination of factors that nurture the mind, consciousness, as well as the actual physiological organ, the brain. Some psychological traits we see in the healthy brain are high maturation, self-awareness, focus, emotional balance, strong memory, resilience, and adaptability.

There are countless books written about motivation. Many of us will buy motivational tapes with the hope that they will keep inspiring us to remain focused on goals and persist even when boredom wants to creep in. Well brains seem to know how to set a goal, rev up the engines, and fire "go." There is clarity and focus, and the brain has been taught how to produce enough dopamine to get the engines roaring.

Creating a to-do list in the morning (or even the day before) is a way to create a road map for the day. Keeping the car gassed up is important because then it can take you to your destination. The drive to get to your destination can be full of beautiful distractions that can stop you along the way; you want to be certain you keep your eyes on the road and get to your destination, your goal!

Interruptions can be so hedonistic and pleasure-filled! The well brain is able to delay gratification, keep its mind on the prize, and steer the car toward the intended goal. Research studies in psychology have shown that the ability to delay gratification is the trait that makes a person most successful and happy in life. This is in contrast to the myth that high self-esteem contributes most to a successful life.

Self-Awareness

Interruptions are able to have power over us if we have not created the self-awareness to be intentional in our goals. This self-awareness is another key component of a well brain. Tuning into one's self can be such a challenging task in today's buzzing world where everybody and everything seems to be conspiring to rob us of silence and mindfulness.

Our minds are becoming full with nonsensical chatter about irrelevant issues versus our minds being guided and filled with what matters the most: empathy, love, kindness, and compassion.

Being self-aware requires a dialing into one's self, an attunement with self, particularly with emotional knowledge. Feelings are the pathway for us to get to know ourselves. A self-aware person is mindful and authentic with their insides and outsides matching. Most of us have a public persona and a private persona. For the self-aware person, the disparity between these two is not that huge, so there is an internal congruity.

A deep understanding of why things happen the way they do in your life is another trait of the self-aware person. When one is able to connect the dots with experiences, emotions, and events that contributed to their life and how best to maximize outcomes, that is a power brain in process! Psychological mindedness appears to present itself in a region of the brain called the insula. It integrates the thinking and feeling parts of our experiences.

People who are regular meditators have well-developed neural circulatory in the insula. The self-aware person can cultivate mindfulness, which is the ability to be in the present without any judgment or criticalness. This detached observation of self is a state that can be trained into our brain with the results being a nonreactive, calm, and emotionally grounded self.

Emotional Balance

This emotional balance is another trait we find in the thriving, well brain. Our emotions are the pathways for survival for us. They will tell us if something is awry in our world. Learning to name and express emotions is a crucial trait of the thriving, well brain. There are two components to a balanced emotional brain: one is to have the emotions and sense to know how to balance the emotions, and the other is to be able to use those emotions and act in the service of the brain.

The amygdala is the part of the brain from which emotions originate. The latest findings in neuroscience have shown us a much more complex picture of the origins of emotion. A network of brain structures, which include the anterior cingulate cortex (ACC), the orbital frontal region of the prefrontal cortex, and the insula, are all implicated in the production of emotions. We now know that the expression and identification of emotions come from many of a person's brain regions.

Additionally, in these same brain regions we have a network of specialized neurons called mirror neurons. These magical neurons are at the bottom of our experience of empathy, or standing in another person's shoes. When we observe another person's emotions, it activates our own. These mirror neurons allow us to "feel" the experience of the other person. This helps us in self-awareness as well as in emotional regulation.

These empathetic, self-aware, well-regulated brains are able to use their emotions to their advantage. Creating balance with our emotions means that the amygdala is not the boss of our life—we are creating harmony between the thinking and feeling selves. A person who has an emotionally balanced, resilient, well brain is likely to observe a person next to them who is displaying road rage with a detached, calm demeanor. They will know to move out of the way of that person—their survival instinct kicks in! Plus, they may even send a message of loving kindness to them!

Resiliency

Resiliency is the ultimate trait of the balanced, healthy brain. Suffering, obstacles, and roadblocks are an inevitable part of a lived life. People who are resilient tend to be buoyant, bouncing back with determination and grit. This grit is a trait that is very much cultivated, not inborn.

Practice, practice, and more practice with making mistakes, having failures, and cultivating optimism in the face of failure are the ingredients of a well, resilient brain. There is a sense of meaning and purpose that resilient people have in the sense that even though unexpected events come up in their lives, they feel in control of where these events are headed.

The ability to tolerate mistakes and failures and move on to the next task fairly easily is a brain that truly manifests its neuroplasticity. The "agitated" neurons are firing, and our ability to calm and soothe them will be reflected by the adaptability we cultivate in our lives.

When one encounters failure in the face of mastery, there is a challenge that is inherently presented. In an attitude of true mastery, one can perceive failure as a failure of strategy—not failure of self. Strategies can be tried numerous times, and strategies are not a reflection of a self. We can try numerous strategies multiple times if we do not internalize failure.

Well, resilient, emotionally grounded brains seem to know what they can internalize and what they can externalize. A key strategy to master is one where we can externalize. This means that if a friend is rude to you, maybe you don't automatically go to, "What did I do wrong?" Instead, perhaps say to yourself, "She/he must be having a rotten day. I wonder what went wrong with their day?" Developing what psychologists term an "internal locus of control" means that you are the chooser of your life; you grab your life instead of others choosing for you.

Resiliency allows there to be adaptability. We know that our brains are constantly changing. We also know that life is not static. As much as some of us control freaks would like things to be the same day in, day out, this is not realistic. Neuroplasticity is confirmation that the world is not constant. The brain would not need to have the "adaptability" gene if everything in our physical environment were to remain the same.

Every time we have a thought, an emotion, and a corresponding behavior, there is a change in our neural circuitry. This is the essence of our adaptability. At the biological and psychological level, adaptability is what has allowed us to evolve and be the successful species that we humans are. The extra circuits that "light up" our brains are creating extra gray matter in our brains, making our brains denser, super-charged, and thicker.

Research with brain matter has shown that the cortical matter of the brain mass increases in density just after six to eight weeks of meditation. Lazar, a scientist who has studied the brains of meditators, showed how the "brainstorm nuclei" that are responsible for the release of norepinephrine and serotonin increase in thickness. That means increased feelings of happiness, well-being, and contentment. Yoga increases serotonin in your brain—drop the Prozac and get into a downward dog position!

The brain's neuroplasticity presents an amazing power for the brain to reshape itself. Healing often happens through the adaptive process. A well brain keeps reinventing itself by learning new things, taking classes, and constantly evolving. Adapting quickly to change, being able to persevere, allowing failure to feel stimulating, and willingness to change from long-held beliefs are essential traits of a healthy brain.

Finally, two additional traits—focus and memory—play a prominent role in keying the well brain up to its superb performance. Incredibly well brains have the ability to harness their focusing power to remember what is important and relevant and to zero in on a task. One has to have incredibly strong focusing power to attain a goal. Interruptions can be used to their advantage.

The ability to single-task, to be in the moment with one-mindedness, is the hallmark of the optimum well brain. Focus can be reinvested by strategies that a well brain teaches itself. These strategies are deliberately minimizing distractions, owning to the self that a distraction is occurring, and causing the self to get excited in the details of the task being completed.

Mindfulness training has been highly successful in increasing focus, concentration, and memory. The well brain knows how to not encode unnecessary details in the memory data bank. A person repeating a task over and over again understandably enhances memory skills. Bar, a researcher at Harvard Medical School, talked about a proactive brain. This proactive brain uses memory to imagine, stimulate, and predict future events. Memory researchers indicate that imagining the future depends on much of the same neural machinery that is needed for remembering the past. Our proactive brain allows us to predict how certain events are going to unfold based on previous events.

If we try something new every week, this experience kicks a bit of dopamine in our brain and increases our brain's memory power. It could be something as small as trying a new type of fruit. This well brain stimulates its memory and focus by enhancing the neural circuitry so new pathways are being born.

Well brains also have an ability to focus into a detail and zoom into a macro focus. Relaxation is a key to integrating memory and focus. Allow the brain to just be so that it can absorb, integrate, and synthesize is a trait that can be cultivated to create a supercharged, well brain.

Seeking out challenging situations where one can become completely immersed allows the brain to be in a state we call flow. The balance between ability and challenge creates flow. We also know that while boredom can feel like one of the most painful experiences one can have, it is truly the seat of creativity.

The brain's ability to be flexible and adaptable — as well as to flow, memorize, and be motivated — gives us emotional and mental balance and a high degree of self-awareness. When the brain can "see" itself, it is a brain in balance. These crucial traits allow us to live a fully lived, contented, and happy life. The health of the brain gives health to the mind. Deeply immersive experiences are highly invigorating for the brain. Many of these traits can be cultivated if the brain is receiving the appropriate nourishment through wholesome, balanced food.

Many people are not aware of the startling fact that our tiny, three-pound brain consumes 20% of the energy we give our body! The brain is the most metabolically active organ in our entire body. It uses 20% of the body's total oxygen supply and 65% of the body's glucose. This means that to keep the well brain at optimum capacity, one must feed it wholesome, complete nutrients.

To perform well, we have to feed our brain well. In today's confusing world, the definition of "healthy" keeps changing. Diet fads can run us ragged if we follow all of them. Yo-yo weight cycling causes more damage to a person's body than just being slightly overweight.

Food

With rapid industrialization of food, our connection with food production has become highly disconnected. As nutrition and diet fads go, there will be new and extreme ways of eating that people will constantly try. Yes, we do have an emerging farm-to-table movement picking up momentum around the globe.

Over the years, we've seen the emergence of multiple diets: South Beach, Atkins, McDougall, raw, as well as a big trend to vegan and Paleo. However, decades of food production in a mass industrialized manner have created generations of habits that are highly addictive — habits where sugar, additives, food coloring, and salt are substances that the craving brain demands.

In my twenty-eight years of experience with all ranges of eating disorders, the most common theme I see is mass confusion that is cultivated by the food industry that makes people frozen, immobilized, and unconscious about food choices. When we live in a mindless zone, what we are then cultivating is a mindless connection with our body. We rarely pause and pay attention to our real hunger.

Might the hunger be for fresh wholesome vegetables, fruits, meats, and grains that our bodies have not become allergic to? Irritable bowel syndrome (IBS), Crohn's disease, and celiac disease are at an all-time high in westernized countries. Grain has become the staple in so many diets. Is it any wonder that our bodies are showing heightened sensitivity to grains, with gluten being the main culprit?

In these past five years, we have had a peak in food sensitivities, as underscored by many documentaries revealing the contaminants in our food chain. This speaks to the alarm that most of us are feeling about the source of our food supply. We now have the ability to detect all the harmful chemicals that are present in food. The mass industrial food complex is alarming as people move away from whole foods to packaged, convenient foods.

Pharmaceutical Industry

Is it a coincidence that the massive amounts of antidepressants being taken in the West seem to correlate with the industrialized production of food? The brain and our "second brain" (the gut) are so malnourished that we have had to manufacture serotonin to get the brain working more effectively.

Much of this points to our toxic food production, as well as the culture of advertising that has created a disconnect that is so massive that we go on to make more drugs that help us pretend that we are happy. These "happy" chemicals have names that pop into the privacy of our living rooms during our cherished TV shows: Prozac, Abilify, Effexor, Paxil, and Seroquel are as familiar in our homes as Huggies, Legos, Harry Potter, Barbie, GI Joe, and Saran Wrap.

Furthermore, some of the biggest secrets that will not be shared are all of the horrible side effects of these medications, with metabolic syndrome being one of the primary factors driving up the incidence of diabetes.

In 2011, a record $4.02 billion in drug prescriptions were written in the United States. Zoloft and Celexa were the most prescribed, with 264 million prescriptions written. If 264 million people per year were put on these medications, with the knowledge that metabolic syndrome is underreported as a side effect of these medications, how many Americans have been pushed toward prediabetic states via these prescriptions? The current amount for the number of psychotropic medications is $200 billion. That is a huge jump from 2011.

The advertising of these drugs has had a positive effect in one way in that it destigmatizes mental illness. However, the negative impact is huge in terms of the ideas it plants in people's minds. The information on side effects is presented as a lightning-fast blurb that flashes across the screen. If we used the same advertising dollars to sell wholesome, varied, organic, close-to-homegrown food, what impact might it have on health in our country? Imagine the state of joy we could experience in our minds, brains, bodies, and souls!

Nutrition, Inflammation, and Disease

As nutrition and diet fads go, there will be new extreme ways of eating that people will constantly try. If we allow ourselves to keep our lives simple, easy, and stress-free while cultivating closeness to nature, the earth, and food that is grown close to home and without pesticides, we may stand a fighting chance at slowing down the numerous auto-immune conditions that have made the headlines in recent years.

Cancer, obesity, celiac, irritable bowel syndrome (IBS), multiple sclerosis, ALS (amyotrophic lateral sclerosis, or Lou Gehrig's disease), and heart disease are all conditions emerging from inflamed bodies. The various environments we live in contain multiple toxins that our bodies are reacting to. Genetically modified organisms; radiation from cell phones, electronic equipment, and wireless Internet; and pollution from carbon emissions are all colliding to create disease states that are overwhelming our medical system in the Western world.

Similarly, as fast food is entering Asian markets, the rates of heart disease, diabetes, and cancer are spiking exponentially. Exporting the standard American diet is not going to come with any warning labels!

Consuming nutrition that is good for the brain (which makes it good for the body), begs us to limit foods that interfere with healthy brain functioning. Some of these foods include alcohol, sugar, artificial sweeteners, MSG, processed foods, and additives.

Grains such as quinoa are not overfarmed and put in our food source. Quinoa is actually not a grain—it is a complete protein that balances the essential amino acids. Foods rich in amino acids balance the brain. If we all begin the journey of once again preparing our food from scratch, creating a connection through preparation of food, our culture stands a chance to regain some steps we have lost to inflammatory diseases.

Rediscovering Family Time and Play

A family that has meals together three to five times a week is less likely to have any behavioral issues among their children and teens. Preparing food together, talking about the day, sitting together, and saying grace before we eat all seem to have become relics of the past. Imagine this same family finishing the dishes, contemplating getting ready for the next day, and ending the evening with the family taking a walk together.

In this diet-obsessed, thin-driven culture, physical exercise seems to have taken an identity that is warped. We no longer move for the sheer joy of moving. We start schlepping children into ballet classes at ages four or five while pushing them into soccer, baseball, and basketball at age seven. Parents aren't even thinking that it is odd for a ten-year-old to play competitive soccer. This ten-year-old has forgotten how to have down time, be bored, or even know what life might feel like just being home every night.

We have begun to overstimulate our children with scheduled activities from such a young age that children have forgotten about free play. We rarely find neighborhood kids just hanging out and playing unstructured games outside. Garage doors open and close in suburbia with a van full of kids that are being shuttled to the nearest park that might be a half-mile away.

The well brain needs lots of play, movement, activity, and joyful jumping. There are regions of the brain that light up with simple, joyful play. With the thousands of studies we have on exercise and mood, there is no doubt that exercise improves mood.

Exercise is one of the best ways to grow new cells in the memory sector of our brain, the hippocampus. There is increased neurogenesis and rejuvenation of neuronal connections with exercise. Exercise stimulates chemicals known as neural growth factors (NGF), which help strengthen memory. With consistent, moderate exercise, one can retain the ability to recall happy memories longer and more often.

Exercise is even more important for the aging brain. If anything, as one gets older, exercise becomes even better for the aging brain. Consistent, moderate exercise enhances learning and memory, improves the function of the neo-cortex (which comprises 85% of your brain). Exercise also slows down age-related atrophy of the brain. Researchers at UC Irvine have conducted numerous studies that state that "exercise is the number one factor" in sustaining brain health and the ability to make new neurons in the aging brain.

Sleep

The well brain that is able to modulate feelings, food, and exercise also can be a brain that cherishes the value of sleep in its routine of wellness. It seems as we are becoming more technologized, our sleep cycles are suffering. We have turned to shorter and shorter hours of sleep at night. The brain makes about fifty chemicals at night. Sleep is incredibly restorative for the well brain. We all know how sluggish we can feel in a day when we have gone with less than seven or eight hours of sleep.

Our brain can only function at its peak capacity if the brain's and body's cells are repaired from the wear and tear that we experience on a daily basis. Insomnia is a rampant condition that is treated in multiple ways. Prescriptions of Ambien, Lunesta, and other sleep aids are on the rise here in the United States. Furthermore, over-the-counter sleep aids sell like hotcakes to an overworked, overstressed clientele that typically burns the candle at both ends.

Our entire well-being is sabotaged if we don't get enough rest. A well-rested, well brain functions smoothly, efficiently, and purrs like a well-oiled engine. Sleep deprivation slows down our brains, increases blood pressure and cholesterol, increases stress hormones (cortisol), and contributes to being overweight.

The brain loves REM sleep! This stage of sleep, which stands for rapid eye movement, comes last during the sleep cycle and is the best sleep for brain function. During REM sleep, the brain is consolidating all of the information it has learned during the day. During REM sleep, the supplies of neurotransmitters are replenished, especially dopamine and serotonin. The final thing that REM sleep does in order to create the well brain is to form neuronal connections that strengthen and form memories. It seems that it is REM sleep that increases the connectivity and plasticity in the brain.

REM sleep is also our dream stage, with the brain having the knowledge on how to use REM sleep to its advantage. The phenomenon of lucid dreaming allows us to train our brain to dream what we want it to dream. This proactive management of our sleep can also be accomplished by cultivating good sleep hygiene habits.

Alcohol consumption, intense exercise before bedtime, a heavy meal, and video gaming and other screen time disrupt our sleep routines and the quality of our sleep. With more than 60 million Americans suffering from insomnia, sleep attention is critical for a healthy brain.

The brain thrives on consistency of bedtime and mellower evening stimulation, so restful sleep can ensue. The calmer, rested mind can also be achieved by practice from mindfulness traditions. Meditation and sympathy are tools the brain knows how to automatically seek out.

Calm, peace, joy, contentment, satisfaction, bliss, and enlightenment emerge from the well brain when there is a healthy balance of emotion regulation, physical exercise, awesome nutrition, sleep, and the knowledge that there is meaning and purpose in life.

Spirituality is a trait that seems to distinguish well brains. We, of course, are not talking about a specific religion. We are really discussing elements within the brain that give us the sense that we are in flow. Synchronicity, peace, calm, joy, and Being are some descriptions we can use to describe the well brain that is harnessing its spirituality. Bursts of insight and creativity, those that we term "a-ha" moments, often come unbridled to a mind that is being prepared. One of the classic ways one prepares the brain, especially the mind for this state of enlightenment, is by meditation.

The spiritual well brain is attuned, empathetic, and feels connected to all beings, sentient and insentient. These people have a sense of calm and detachment with mental clarity that is admirable. When one operates with clarity, detachment, and calm, we are less swayed by others' opinions, allowing us to become more truthful. As a result of the heightened mirror neurons we discussed earlier, this empathetic person feels deeper love, connection, and resonance within their world.

Mindfulness training is one of the primary ways in which we can "tune" our brain. Yoga, mindfulness, and brain training have inundated our culture in this last decade. Neuroscientists are becoming some of our most-respected leaders in this discipline, and I expect this decade to be called the "golden age of the brain."

Human beings have the brain power and the brain sophistication to view the brain itself. We do not know if other animals are able to observe their own thoughts. Andrew Newberg, M.D., the Director of Research of the Marcus Institute of Integrative Health in Philadelphia, is spearheading the emerging field of neurotheology, which researches what happens in the brain during religious and spiritual experiences. Mario Beauregard, a neuroscientist from the University of Montreal and author of *The Spiritual Brain*, continues to conduct excellent research in the field of spirituality and brain science.

Mystical experiences (MEs) and near-death experiences (NDEs) are being researched by these neuroscientists. Of course, their findings do not uncover a "God spot" or "God module" in the brain. They have found a fascinating discovery, that the regions of the brain that are activated by people who experience these MEs are in the temporal lobe and other brain regions implicated in perception, positive emotions, body representation within space, and self-consciousness. Different types of spiritual experiences are associated with distinct brain areas and networks.

Mindfulness, prayer, and meditation allow us to fine-tune our consciousness so that our brains can serve us better. The well brain resides comfortably in the knowledge that consciousness now comes first, and then comes the brain with all its bells and whistles.

The most powerful effect of a well-trained, conscious mind is the sense of oneness with the Whole. There is no duality, no separateness, and all beings are interconnected with everything in the Universe. We are not powerless, biochemical machines. The manner in which we guide our mind creates states of ease or disease in our souls, psyches, and bodies.

When we "act" as if God is real, then we are able to operate from a place where we are open, receptive, and see the good in other people. Plus, we become flexible in our encounters in our world. We are mindfully present in each moment and fully experience joy each day.

Anger, envy, greed, and jealousy become emotions that we feel more in control of because we have the ability to be compassionate with ourselves. The empathy that is cultivated from this self and other feelings of compassion have the ability to create a life force around us that gives us serenity, emotional generosity, and a feeling of connection and belonging.

Meditative practices have been proven to change the actual structure of the brain. Similarly, we find that neurofeedback as a brain training methodology is able to change the structure of the brain. Neurofeedback is a potent tool that allows us to deliberately change what is going on in our brain.

Mario Beauregard describes it as a "psycho-neuro technology" that gives us a glimpse into the remarkable power of our minds. As we discovered earlier, neurofeedback enhances a person's cognitive functions, reduces anxiety, and improves mood. This enhanced sense of well-being is able to leave psychic energy available for a person to explore states of being that are beyond survival.

Many of us practitioners of neurofeedback have anecdotal stories we share about our patients who experience transcendental experiences. Neurofeedback technology is rapidly evolving, with neurofeedback practitioners becoming more adept at controlling activities in specific regions of the brain. The further refinement of this technology has tremendous implications for psycho-neurotherapists, psychologists, psychiatrists, neurologists, neurosurgeons, and, of course, meditation masters.

CHAPTER 5

ATHLETES AND NEUROFEEDBACK: PEAK PERFORMANCE

Each point I play is in the now moment. The last point means nothing, the next point means nothing.

~ Billie Jean King

EVERY ATHLETE WILL TELL US that to play an entire game in the present moment is the ultimate in mental discipline. Managers, coaches, and trainers spend countless hours teaching their athletes to be in the "zone." Successful athletes will often speak of playing the zone. What they are describing is a calm mind that is fully present, in the moment, with mind and body fully attuned to each other. They are not aware of any distractions around them, with their mind completely dialed into the goal they want to attain.

Athletes will be the first to state that mental and emotional conditioning is just as important as physical conditioning. Chris Evert, the number-one tennis player who won 18 grand slam championships, believes that her weapons for winning were her concentration, competitive spirit, confidence, fitness, and poise under pressure. She believes she won because she could compete better, with her greatest strength being tough thinking.

Sports psychologists and neurofeedback therapists work in concert to create a mind and a brain that cultivate this intense focus, mental balance, and ability to have control over emotions so that the game remains a mental game of toughness. This is where neurofeedback plays a profoundly significant role in the training of the athlete's brain.

James Loehr, a premier sports psychologist, describes the real markers of toughness that he believes are crucial to the success of an athlete. These are: emotional flexibility, emotional responsiveness, emotional strength, and emotional resiliency.

Neuroscience, coupled with our ability to measure brain waves of athletes, has given us excellent data we can work with that allows us to know how to train an athlete into their peak brain zone for optimum performance. Many athletes are beginning to work with a neurotherapist who is also equipped to conduct a brain map called QEEG. QEEG measures the brainwave activity in all regions of the brain, giving very specific clues to the areas that need performance enhancement. This is enhancement without any steroids!

Peak performance training is conducted with athletes who may already be at the top of their game and want the extra advantage. One of an athlete's worst fears is to choke under the pressure of a tight moment in a game. Other athletes may come to neurofeedback after they realize that their recovery time from an error is impairing their performance.

Yet others can be keenly aware that extra pressure may have a tendency of forcing them out of their zone, thereby spiraling their game downward. Athletes can also tend to overanalyze their games and errors, which can lead to the brain getting stuck—what they call paralysis by analysis. Perfectionism is a trait that can be both an asset and a liability.

The well brain that was discussed earlier is akin to the highly performing athlete's brain. The "zone" is an essence of athletic experience, very similar to an experience of transcendence where the athlete is not fighting against themselves, they are not afraid, and they are living in a moment — in a special place and time. Some use the phrases "flow, peak experiences, being on autopilot, white moments, or being in the bubble." When an athlete can command this zone at their fingertips, they are then in control of their game to the quintessential degree. Neurofeedback is one of the most successful tools that can bring an athlete to the zone.

What is this state, the zone, you may ask? There seem to be some common characteristics and traits. Susan Jackson presented a few conditions that may allow us to reach the zone by controlling the mind.

Balance is a condition in which an athlete has to experience the optimum amount of challenge for the skill sets that are currently present in that athlete. It is really less about the actual talent, and more about the perception of that talent. What we think we can achieve will determine our experience and outcome more than our actual abilities will. To change our perceptions requires self-confidence. The athlete has to think about their successes rather than their failures. Anxiety and boredom can both block the zone.

Total absorption is a state whereby there is a cohesive and balanced fusion between action and consciousness. This unification creates a balance between the mental and physical processes and the acute awareness, resulting in perfect timing.

A critical component of any high-performance task requires clarity. It is important to have clear goals. Athletes are trained to link these goals with words, feelings, pictures of successes, and particularly the action. This clarity helps the athlete remove any clutter from their mind.

Another important trait that enhances being in the zone is how the athlete uses feedback. This feedback can be from their own kinesthetic performance — their body movements. This internal feedback loop gives the athlete instantaneous, real-time information that allows them to return to an optimum level. This feedback can, of course, come from coaches, peers, and family as well.

Through repetition and training, the brain learns to filter out information that can overwhelm it. The entire backbone of being in the zone is concentration. English golfer Tony Jacklin, a 2002 inductee into the World Golf Hall of Fame, calls this total immersion, "a cocoon of concentration."

An athlete's ability to stay focused on the present by concentrating on the action, ignoring what has previously happened, and not anticipating outcomes is the total immersion of successful concentration. Furthermore, cognitive flexibility is also required in this total concentration, where the athlete may have to quickly shift focus if the game or environment is suddenly changing.

A sense of control is another component of the zone. An athlete who feels totally in control feels a sense of mastery, competency, and knowledge that the task is feasible. There is a feeling of power, confidence, and calm that comes with this feeling or state.

This sense of control allows the athlete to put aside feelings of doubt, fatigue, and self-consciousness. By this point, every athlete also knows they want to have fun in their sport!

The most intriguing trait of being in the zone is the motion of time and space being suspended. Athletes will describe it in words like, "Everything seemed slower, so there is more time to adjust." NBA legend Bill Walton is reported to have said, "Everything slows down. It's like everybody is wearing cement shoes, the ball is in motion, and everything slows down except you. You feel like you are operating at a different speed and at a different level than everybody else."

This modified state of consciousness appears to be similar in theme to the "a-ha" moments, mystical experiences, or transcendence experiences frequently described in spiritual readings. This is also a state that is able to be induced by the Alpha/Theta training module of neurofeedback.

Visualization, the ability to think creatively, cultivating positive thoughts, and feeling good about one's self all enhance the ability to go into the zone. Many athletes also report having an ability to mobilize high energy even in the face of fatigue.

Brain training with neurofeedback allows the brain to maintain intensity and focus, especially under conditions of adversity. The body might try telling the mind to stop, but the mind, because it is so finely tuned, asks the body to continue. This doesn't make sense. The brain training allows the various regions in the brain to communicate more effectively with each other. The result of this is a turbocharged, focused, energetic, driven, calm, and balanced brain.

It is imperative to remember that there is a dark side to the zone, where the mind and body are so segregated that an athlete keeps pushing until they collapse. Dr. John Douillard, a sports psychologist, discusses the existence of two different experiences of the zone. One comes from integration and harmony between mind and body, and the other from a breakdown between the two. He gave the example of an ultra-marathoner through a 100-mile endurance run where runners frequently collapse.

Exhaustion can be so severe that the body produces a ton of endorphins, enkephalins, plus other morphine-like substances, where it does more than kill the pain. As the mind is swimming in the pool of morphine, it becomes numb to the body. A clearer definition of this toughness is imperative so that an athlete trains herself/himself from entering the dark side of the zone.

A combination of talent, skill, and toughness come together to create achievement in a sport. Both talent and skill are important with Dr. Loehr, who is a sports psychologist and has written about toughness training in sports, believes that toughness is the most important trait to cultivate. He defines toughness as "the ability to consistently perform toward the upper range of your talent and skill, regardless of competitive circumstances."

There are four building blocks of toughness that neurofeedback practitioners have to understand as they work with athletes. It is imperative that we have a clean understanding of toughness being **emotional flexibility, emotional responsiveness, emotional strength**, and **emotional resilience**.

The athlete has to cultivate very disciplined thinking and the ability to act under stress. Coaches and trainers work very closely with an athlete in administering just the right amount of stress so that the tension creates a growth curve.

Every athlete experiences some level of physical, mental, and emotional stress as they cultivate their toughness. Physical stress is obvious: running, hitting, jumping, weight lifting, walking, moving, and exercising. Mental stress incorporates thinking, concentrating, focusing, visualizing, imaging, analyzing, and problem-solving. Finally, emotional stress would be in the arena of feeling angry, feeling fearful, sad, depressed, negative, frustrated, and hurt.

It is in this building block of toughness where neurofeedback plays the most important role with athletes. Recovery from this stress is a critical part of the athlete being able to bounce back, have resiliency, and continue to perform at their peak.

Neurofeedback is a personally tailored system that allows the athlete to see directly which brain waves need regulation. The brain is retrained and reconditioned. Numerous research studies are being conducted with athletes with a clear delineation being established. Different sports activities have varying demands placed on different regions of the brain. There is no one-size-fits-all brain training for all sports.

Neurofeedback also holds potential for improving athletic performance by helping improve physical balance. Imagine the benefits in sports like gymnastics, skiing, ice skating, hockey, skateboarding, snowboarding, ballet, tennis, martial arts, basketball, baseball, and football.

Typically, with issues related to balance, neurofeedback training can be as short as eight to ten sessions with marked improvement being experienced. It has become commonplace for many elite teams to incorporate neurofeedback into their training schedule. AC Milan players gather every two weeks in the "Mind Room," which is their Neurofeedback Center. As we presented earlier, the brain "talks" through the wavelengths of its electrical currents: Alpha and SMR (relaxed openness and focus), Beta (multitasking efficient, anxiety, and mind chatter), and Theta (wandering mind). The core tenet of neurofeedback, then, is that when we observe our brainwaves and see how we want to change them, with guided training, we can take them to maximize performance and function.

Phil Jackson, one of the greatest coaches of our time, incorporated mindfulness, meditation, and Zen practices in coaching the NBA's Chicago Bulls. He was heavily influenced by Eastern meditation practices in college, especially Buddhism, and by Native American wisdom as well. When he describes his approach to coaching, Jackson says, "It encompasses the attitude that Zen is a way to integrate mind and body, sport and spiritual." When have we ever heard a coach of successful teams talk about spirituality and athletics?

Jackson is a daily meditator himself and introduced it into his daily coaching. The team knew that they would all do group meditation, sitting still quietly and focusing on their breathing. Jackson was known to buy meditation books for his players, exposing them to the wide-open, uncharted territory of their brains, which is an open canvas for them to paint on!

The meditation cultivates the brain in the same way that neurofeedback gets the brain ready to be in the zone. Attention to detail, sharp focus, and an ability to see the big picture, can only be done by a brain that is cultivating its neuroplasticity. When a team is doing a group meditation together, they have the intense feeling of connectedness, Oneness, and synchronicity. The inner harmony is experienced by the enhanced intuition each player would have regarding the other players on the team. Anticipating, sensing, connecting, and the quickness of mental processes are major elements of what made Phil Jackson's team the envy of the NBA, with eleven championships.

Imagine the potential we have with neurofeedback with the injuries that occur to football and ice hockey players. The brain injuries suffered by players in these tough contact sports can be corrected by neurofeedback *only* if neurofeedback becomes a standard of care for these poor souls whose brains get banged about every single day they are out there on the field or the ice.

Neurofeedback offers tremendous implications for athletes from all ranges of sports. Not only can it help with Peak Performance Training, but it can also help with injured athletes, particularly when there is brain damage. The frontier for brain training in athletics is just dawning. Olympic teams have begun to use neurofeedback in the last four to six years. Most tend to be secretive about their use because they don't want their competitors to have an advantage over them.

Lucas Giolito of the MLB's Chicago White Sox recently spoke eloquently about how twenty sessions of neurofeedback training in the off-season took him to a level of focus and performance in his sagging career, which enabled him to become an All-Star pitcher in 2019. He directly attributes his success to neurofeedback.

MLB infielder Brian Barden was looking to reduce his distractions and eliminate self-destructive thoughts. He enlisted the help of Dr. Silverman, a Scottsdale psychologist who conducted neurofeedback sessions on him. His game improved dramatically. Numerous football teams also use neurofeedback as a tool for peak performance enhancement.

In this next decade, we are definitely going to see neurofeedback making headlines in the sports world. An increasing number of athletes are aware that their minds can get in the way of their optimum performance, so we anticipate seeing people flocking to our centers in droves.

CHAPTER 6

CEOs AND NEUROFEEDBACK: OPTIMIZING PRODUCTIVITY

Management is doing things right;
Leadership is doing the right things.

~ Peter Drucker

A SUCCESSFUL CEO has to have vision, innate personal power, and leadership as part of their nature. Leading should feel like an integral part of their *being* in the world. Leaders who have vision and personal power tend to be leaders with integrity and are not afraid to take risks that make them unpopular.

A number of skill sets, perspectives, and views of the world define how a leader can successfully lead a team to productivity. A leader has to be willing to think outside the box and look at novel ways in which productivity in a company can be enhanced. Perhaps one of the most important skill sets that has not been emphasized in corporations is "mindsight." CEOs tend not to focus on the most important commodity that makes a workplace highly successful. This commodity is the brain, the brain of the CEO and that of their employees.

The brain is an amazing organ. It is *the* primary organ that gives us that incredible feeling of accomplishment, gratification, and contentment all at the same time. It is instrumental in making an employee rise to the top by the choices it helps the person make, enhancing the productivity of the entire company. In essence, the success of a company depends on how fine-tuned the "brains" of the company are.

The organ that uses 20% of our energy resources of the day, and resting between the ears, can often be the organ that is most neglected by CEOs. Very few business schools have courses in neuroscience where the biology behind motivation, drive, habits, and performance is taught. The frontier of brain science is at a very exciting place; amazing new information is being presented to us every day, which can help make the brain healthier, more efficient, and much more productive with the least amount of stress.

Neuroplasticity, one of the most radical discoveries of this decade, has revolutionized our ways of thinking about the mind, the brain, the body and, ultimately, our performance. Neuroplasticity gives us a much more acute understanding of how the brain works. Many scientists believe that the sensory map imprinted on the brain forms rudimentary consciousness and the next stage of the development of mirror neurons.

Mirror neurons were first described and discovered in monkeys in the 1990s, and it was only in 2010 that they were formally identified in humans. Vilaynayur Ramachandran, a neuroscientist at UC San Diego, predicts that the discovery of "mirror neurons" will do for psychology what DNA did for biology.

Mirror neurons tell us that human beings are first and foremost mimics. We make ourselves up as we go along by improvising from what we see. The self is really in dynamic interaction with otherness, both copying behavior and projecting its emotions onto others, which is the essence of empathy. This mirror neuron system enables us to see another person's point of view, as opposed to an egocentric, self-centered view.

Some other examples of mirror neurons working are when we feel a need to yawn when someone else is yawning, or when you may get hungry when you see someone eating even if you just had a meal an hour ago!

Our brains are influenced by just watching someone else's actions. Imagine the power that CEOs have in their companies. If a CEO is actively engaged in compassion, meditation, and mindfulness work, her roots of empathy will be deep. The application for neurofeedback is significant since it has the potential to teach empathy. It is not a difficult conjecture to make when we state that as a brain learns to cultivate empathy for itself via neurofeedback, then neurofeedback is creating more mirror neuron pathways.

The way mirror neurons work is that when we see an act and we understand the purpose of the act, we ready ourselves to mirror it. At the simplest level, that's why we get thirsty when others drink and look up when others do. This could explain why a younger sibling is often better at sports than the older one.

This sibling has watched hours and hours of the older sibling playing, so their mirror neurons have fixed each time their older sibling has pitched a ball or kicked a soccer ball. At the most complex level, these mirror neurons help us understand the nature of culture and how our shared behaviors bind us together, child to parent, friend to friend, spouse to spouse, and boss to employee.

Mirror neurons not only help us imitate behaviors, but they also help us emulate emotional states. Mirror neurons are at the crux of us being able to resonate with the feelings and emotional states of others. Dan Siegel calls these neurons "sponge neurons" because we soak up the behaviors, intentions, and emotions of someone else like a sponge. We don't just "mirror back" to someone else, but we "sponge in" their internal states. Scientists also have another word for it, which is "emotional contagion."

So, we can see how the brain is a totally social organ. We soak in other people into our inner world. Our biology is made for social relationships, to understand where other people are coming from and to influence each other.

These advances in neuroscience may help us understand the internal mechanisms that enable some people to be effective leaders, and some not. Leaders engage and inspire others — that is how a CEO can get the company to move forward. For the last century, we have been studying the personality, intelligence, values, attributes, and behaviors of leaders in order to understand a successful visionary from an unsuccessful one.

It is extremely rare for any scientists to have entered the physiology of the brains of CEOs. Advances in fMRIs (functional magnetic resonance imaging), which show regions of brains that are activated with tasks and/or social interactions, are all tools that give us huge insights into the effectiveness of CEOs.

An exploratory study was conducted by organizational theorist Richard Boyatzis. He and his team wanted to examine what happens in the brains of people as they recall certain critical incidents with their leaders/bosses. They hypothesized that when these individuals had resonant leaders, their brains would show certain types of activation. The fascinating findings were that for these employees who had resonant leaders (i.e., empathetic, valuing relationships), fourteen regions of interest were activated in the brain, while dissonant leaders only activated six and deactivated eleven regions. Resonant leaders activated more focus, attention, empathy, and safety in relationships. Non-resonant leaders activated narrowing of attention, tunnel vision, less compassion, and more negative emotions. Dissonant leaders turn people off who lose their motivation and then productivity falls dramatically.

We spend one-third of our lives in the workplace, so the relationships with our leaders, CEOs, and colleagues are instrumental in shaping our brains. A CEO who is results-driven is not going to create the same kind of productivity as a CEO who is relationship-driven.

John Chambers, the former CEO of Cisco Systems, and Oprah Winfrey of Harpo Productions are both driven to produce impressive results. But when people who work directly with them talk about their meetings, they describe walking out feeling motivated and inspired by what they are doing, which reinforces their commitment to each other and to the company.

Furthermore, studies have been conducted on examining how very little time it takes for an employee to react to a

CEO's bad mood, which creates a rapid downward spiral. Our unconscious emotional states are arousing emotions in those with whom we interact before we or they even know it—and it spreads from these interactions to others.

The contagion factor of negative emotions is stronger than that of positive emotions. When negative feelings are aroused, the sympathetic nervous system is activated, which quickly leads to the fight–flight–freeze response. Positive emotions, on the other hand, activate the parasympathetic nervous system, which stimulates adult neurogenesis (growth of neurons), a sense of well-being, improved immune system functioning, and cognitive, emotional, and perceptual openness.

In short, CEOs have a tremendous effect on the neuroplasticity of their employees. Imagine that each CEO was taught to visualize how their tiny interaction with their employee either creates a positive neural pathway or a negative one! The implication of the study of neuroscience as it relates to mirror neurons is that leaders bear the primary responsibility for knowing what they are feeling and thinking. As a result, they can manage the contagion they have the potential to create in their employees. This type of self-awareness is what Google has created in their work environment through the SIY (Search Inside Yourself) program.

The SIY program was created by Chede-Meng Tan and to date, over one thousand Google employees have experienced the program. It is a mindfulness-based emotional intelligence program, which is rooted in science that delivers improvements in productivity, collaboration, and engagement.

The program can be brought to your company, and it helps organizations develop leaders that are focused, creative, and resilient. They do this by providing practical tools for daily use to support a positive, engaged, and innovative workplace culture. Their main tenet is the creation of leadership, efficiency, and happiness in a corporation. Which MBA program teaches about creating happiness in the workplace? It is usually all about productivity.

Managers, CEOs, and leaders need to have heightened self-awareness. Neurofeedback in particular has a protocol called Alpha/Theta that works to expand the awareness of the person and increase their empathy. The mental chatter that can be caused in the brain by excessive Beta waves can be controlled with neurofeedback, resulting in a calm, alert, and focused mind. Leaders with calm, alert, and focused minds make better decisions, allowing their companies to prosper.

"Mindsight" or "mind awareness" is a key element that an excellent CEO possesses. Having techniques that help a CEO recognize they are having a feeling, to be able to name it, understand it, and describe it should be the standard that every emerging CEO cultivates. Trying to put on a happy face is unsuccessful because we can see how quickly employees pick up on negative emotions from their supervisors.

It is imperative that CEOs become aware that they are "infecting" others with specific feelings. Some of these feelings can help their employees perform better and innovate, and others can be debilitating and stop adoptive thinking. The leader, because of their position of power, has a great impact on others in social or work environments. Being able to change their internal state may be one of the most powerful techniques a CEO can learn in becoming an effective leader—one who inspires others to learn, adopt, and perform their best.

Many coaches are unaware of the fact that one of the best ways to coach and employee is with compassion. The resonance that is created with compassion is far superior to the more common results-oriented type of coaching. It is known that with neurofeedback, the brain can be tuned to a state of peak performance where agitation is reduced, the mind is clear, and emotions are calm. If the CEO utilizes neurofeedback as one of the strategies or methods in his or her toolkit, then the manner in which they coach would be much more mindful, creating positive, inspired energy in the staff.

These mindful CEOs are able to do their best on their worst day. They also see creativity as a result of *effort*, not inspiration. This effort can be toiling, striving, reforming, testing, and experimentation. Another way they achieve extraordinary productivity is that they accept fear as a part of the deal. When they fail, they find the strength to keep moving forward.

Because they have active mirror neurons and they are socially connected, they see help as essential and not a weakness. Ultimately, they start their projects and focus on how they will feel when they are finished; they try not to think about the pain of the task.

The implications for the types of leadership are that CEO can learn how to activate the part of the brain that some researchers call PEA (Positive Emotional Attractor).

In a test to see how various coaching styles affect performance, Boyatzis divided a group of students into two different coaching paradigms. One was PEA, which is coaching with compassion and asking the person about their dreams and aspirations. The other coaching style was NEA (Negative Emotional Attractor), where the students were asked how they are handling their courses and whether they are doing all of their homework. They tracked the brains of these students using fMRI technology and found dramatic results.

The NEA activated the anterior circulate cortex (ACC) and medial prefrontal cortex, which are areas that are activated when we feel anxious and guilty. The PEA activated the visual cortex and orbitofrontal cortex (OFC). The OFC is involved in thoughtful, mindful decision-making processes. Damage to this area makes people impulsive. People that are prone to drug addictions and alcoholism have damage to their OFC.

Boyatzis's findings correlated with those by other researchers Jack, Dewson, and group, which showed that when one is engaged in social activities, there is a completely different network that is activated than when you are engaged in analytics or solving a nonsocial problem. So when we are busy thinking about financials, budgets, or product specifications, you will have turned off parts of your brain that are key to social functioning and vice versa.

The bottom line of what this recent research suggests is that CEOs will be much more influential in a positive way if they are social and engaged, and if they nurture mindful contemplation in their employees. When used for this type of peak performance, neurofeedback can be one of the best tools a CEO can bring into their company.

I have a vision of each corporation having half-hour slots available at neurofeedback booths where employees can come in during a break and plug themselves onto a machine that is so well-automated that it can be self-run. The US would become once again a giant in productivity, creativity, and sales.

Considering that neurofeedback is considered level 1 treatment for ADHD and ADD, just treating that segment of employees in a company can boost productivity by 50%. Scattered and frazzled employees would begin and finish projects on time and can establish realistic timelines for themselves, which would help increase the bottom line and productivity.

Loss of productivity through issue of attention can create huge losses for a company. Attention-training exercises such as neurofeedback, mindfulness, and meditation are proving to recreate focus, clarity, creativity, and follow-through on projects. Aware, mindful colleagues create a compassionate, team-oriented, cohesive work culture that emphasizes collective growth versus a competitive, individualistic focus. Numerous studies reveal that collaborative work styles are more productive and successful.

Addictions can also be a huge source of loss of revenue in companies. If a person is gambling, drinking, or is addicted to Internet pornography, it is very likely that they are going to be a preoccupied and unproductive employee. Neuro-feedback has been successful in treating addictions and creating neurogenesis in the brain, which ultimately leads to a more balanced brain. More balanced brains directly make a company more balanced.

The costs of treating addictions and the loss of revenue in our country are outrageously high. Neurofeedback is not talk therapy, and many men and women are more receptive to rebooting and rewiring their brains than talking about their feelings. This can be a very successful way to regulate an employee who is having alcohol and addiction problems; EAP centers would benefit from having staff that is trained in neurofeedback.

The numbers of employees that are on medications would drop dramatically, which can save many thousands of dollars for the corporation in health care benefits. A well corporation creates well employees, and wellness can be created in a multitude of ways, with neurofeedback being a cornerstone of this wellness.

CHAPTER 7

TAKE CHARGE OF YOUR BRAIN: ACHIEVING OPTIMUM BRAIN FITNESS

*Learn from yesterday, live for today, hope for tomorrow.
The important thing is not to stop questioning.*

~ Albert Einstein

IN THIS INCREDIBLE ERA of brain science, research, and technology, neurogenesis is the most exciting, rewarding, and enriching liberator. As you have read through the chapters of this book, my hope is that your awareness has increased exponentially about how incredibly supercharged *you* can make your brain. This CEO of our body has given us deep insights on what makes it work in the most optimum way.

Neurons are the building blocks of our superhighway of the brain. The health of each neuron creates health in the brain. A healthy brain creates a healthy body. A healthy body creates a healthy organism, which then creates a healthy community. Most importantly, a healthy brain creates a healthy mind. An optimum mind and brain then really become the building blocks of a committed, empathetic, focused community.

Optimum brain fitness has ramifications that are more far-reaching than just delaying Alzheimer's, dementia, or strategies to combat memory issues. Optimum brain function could actually elevate us to a higher ground of mindfulness and being, which has the potential to create calm amid chaos.

The brain's primary way of growth is by adding synapses in the neurons. The stimulation of the electrical impulses via neurofeedback increases the blood flow to the brain, bolstering the highways that are being built in the brain.

Neurogenesis, the growth of new neurons in the brain, is a process that we all need to grasp in its entirety. There are highly specific things we can do to increase the health of the brain, and this is a concept that is *not* talked about enough. We can and we *must* treat the brain well so that it gives us the happiness and joy we want in life.

How many books on happiness are there in bookstores and on Amazon? Do any of them say anything about taking care of the most important organ in our body — the brain? This is a tragedy that has to be corrected by the way we educate those around us. There are very specific, highly successful lifestyle changes that can help us nurture the brain. Growing a brain can be a very exciting process, and the good news is that it is never too late to start!

This section will help you take baby steps that will help you to start prioritizing what you can begin to do on a daily basis. Exercise, quality and quantity of food, sleep, meditation, memory training, neurofeedback, optimism, DHA, BDNF, and learning new things are just some of the brain enhancers we'll discuss.

Furthermore, we'll also look at brain drainers or brain shrinkers that are mental, physical, and environmental. Some of these brain drainers are insomnia, anxiety, depression, stroke, traumatic brain injury, alcohol, sleep apnea, inflammation, obesity, cell phones, technology, video games, social media, stress, and environmental toxins we take in from chemicals, wheat, at the cleaners, and through electro-magnetic radiation.

Exercise

Our human brain is an incredibly malleable organ. Exercise is one of the activities with the most direct effect on the brain. Numerous studies have shown the amazing impact that happens to the growth of the hippocampus after just three months of consistent exercise three or four times per week. If you remember, the hippocampus in the brain is an extremely important organ in that it is the storehouse for memory. Exercise increases the size of the brain. Children and teens who exercise regularly have hippocampi that are 12% larger than those of their unfit peers. The developing brain really thrives on exercise. The cortex, too, grows as a person exercises more.

Studies have shown that those who exercised regularly (walking or running about six to nine miles a week) had significantly more gray matter in the frontal, occipital, and hippocampal regions than those who walked less. Denser gray matter in the brain makes for a more efficient brain. You want more gray matter in your brain. That means you have more neurons and more neurons that are interconnected. The interconnectivity of the neurons makes the brain more alert, sharper, and focused.

Exactly how does exercise help the brain? Believe it or not, we have a substance that is a brain fertilizer: BDNF (Brain-Derived Neurotrophic Factor), the neurochemical that health practitioners are buzzing about. Neuroscientists are currently putting a ton of time and research into exploring all the nuances of BDNF. They are looking at what produces more of it, how to influence its production, and the exciting way it creates neurogenesis in the brain.

Vigorous, intense exercise immediately increases the levels of BDNF in the brain. Exercise starts by helping the cardiovascular network, increasing blood flow to all organs of the body. When blood is flowing more easily into the body, the vessels bathe the body with oxygen. The extra oxygen coupled with better blood flow to the whole body makes the brain a much more finely tuned organ.

The science that informs us about the prevention of cognitive decline is stunning when it presents the role of exercise! Aerobic exercise increases BDNF, reverses memory decline, and makes new brain cells. Another amazing advantage of exercise is that it increases the alpha wave activity in the brain. This alpha activity is the relaxed, focused state. The increased levels of endorphins and dopamine increase the alpha brainwave activity.

Quality and Quantity of Food and Nutrients

Creation of these new brain cells can only be effective to the degree to which we feed these cells with the best possible nutrients. Food, the second enhancer, plays just as important of a role as exercise does for optimum brain fitness. The rapid industrialization of food from the 1940s and '50s is one of the biggest factors contributing to cognitive decline that we are seeing, with millions of people being diagnosed with Alzheimer's disease in our country.

We are all hearing a lot about super foods, antioxidants, and brain foods, which easily create a feeling of being overwhelmed. It seems that mass media is constantly on the hunt for the newest and best diet. So much of the focus has been on dieting to lose weight that we have completely lost connection with the organ that uses the most amount of energy in our body — the brain!

Pound for pound, even with the brain weighing a total of just three pounds, it uses a whopping 25% of the food energy we give it. The quality of food we give the brain truly matters.

With all the confusing information we can tend to receive via journals, magazines, and television, the information presented in this chapter is the latest science-based information collected from numerous reputable sources. For brain health, processed foods have to be stopped. Any prepackaged foods will come with preservatives and coloring added to the food. All these chemicals are brain drainers.

Fresh, wholesome foods are truly the only way to go. Proteins that are organic and farm-fresh products give the brain the best it needs. If you were driving a Ferrari, which is really the brain, would you be putting the cheapest fuel possible in the car?

The origin of brain disease is primarily inactivity and dietary. Inflammation of the brain is being viewed as the primary cause of Alzheimer's. In his amazing book, *Grain Brain*, Dr. David Perlmutter calls Alzheimer's Type 3 diabetes. He attributes the epidemic of Alzheimer's to four factors.

As a silent but deadly brain condition, these folks have lived with chronic high blood sugar levels in the absence of diabetes. Secondly, they have eaten too many carbohydrates over their lifetime. Thirdly, they have chosen a low-fat diet that minimizes cholesterol, and finally — and perhaps most important — is undiagnosed sensitivity to gluten, the protein found in wheat, rye, and barley.

More studies are currently emerging on the connection between gluten insensitivity and neurological dysfunction. The overuse of grains in all our foods has created a sensitivity, such as our bodies becoming inflamed with the amount of grains we consume.

The second critical factor that is highly misunderstood is cholesterol. We have thousands of people who have "high" cholesterol that are on statins, which are cholesterol-lowering drugs. Our brains *need* cholesterol to thrive. Statins reduce brain function and increase the risk for heart disease. Cholesterol is an essential fuel for the neurons. A study published in 2012 in the *Archives of Internal Medicine* documented an astounding 48% increased risk for diabetes among women taking statin medications.

Nutritionally, the following are foods that help the brain tremendously and reduce inflammation of the brain. Omega 3 (DHA) is one of the most protective ingredients we can put in our brain. It needs to be added to the diet because we don't eat sufficient fish or algae to bring it to the levels that are optimum for our brain. DHA has been studied extensively; it enhances learning and improves brain function. It has been used extensively for the treatment of ADHD with tremendous success.

Consuming flavonoids is another beneficial way we can enhance brain function. We teach the patients at our clinic to eat foods that are "all colors of the rainbow." This ensures that we are getting apples, beets, grapes, berries of all kinds, curcumin, spinach, tomatoes, broccoli, and bell peppers. Green tea, black tea, pecans, and pistachios are additional excellent sources of flavonoids. Small quantities of coffee and chocolate enhance brain function as well.

Having the optimum amount of Vitamin D, Vitamin B12, and Vitamin E are also essential to brain health. There is additional research that shows that cholesterol-lowering drugs reduce the amount of CoQ10 that the brain makes available to itself.

CoQ10 is the energy molecule that makes the mitochondria in our cells function more efficiently. As we are, our CoQ10 levels drop and statin drugs reduce the CoQ10 levels in the blood and brain, which then causes neurological dysfunction in the brain. These supplemental vitamins and the enzyme CoQ10 then makes the brain a supercharged turbo engine!

Resveratrol, the substance present in red wine, helps enhance brain function by slowing down the aging process, increasing blood blow to the brain, and curbing fat cells. However, it is critical to note that one glass of wine does not give you enough. Since alcohol does kill neurons in the brain, it is not recommended that you drink more. Instead, a good idea is to take a supplement of 5 mg of resveratrol per day, which is adequate.

Much of this section focuses on quality of food, but quantity of food cannot be ignored. The brain and body function at their best when the body is not overindulged with the amount of food. Size, particularly the midsection area of the belly, has been known to add to inflammation of the body. As an eating disorder psychologist who firmly believes in health at every size model, this section underscores the importance of how dieting deprives the brain of valuable nutrients.

Dieting causes obesity. Our body and brain need fat in our food—high cholesterol is good. Coconut oil is an awesome fat, as are olive oil and avocado! A person can have belly fat even as they are gluten free and have the right "high" cholesterol. Examining gluten's role in being overweight is a critical element that we can pay attention to.

Allowing the body to have the right digestive bacteria is a necessary ingredient of good digestive health. Good digestive balance and health creates satiety, especially when the food is rich, wholesome, fresh, and comes from all colors of the rainbow! Food, mood, and sleep are very much interconnected, so let's examine the necessity of adequate good-quality sleep for the care of the brain.

Sleep

Insomnia is one of the conditions here in the US that accounts for millions of dollars of lost productivity and increased dependence on over-the-counter sleep aids and prescription sleep medications. Prolonged periods of sleep deprivation cause so much havoc in the poor brain that we have got to wake up to the brain drain that is caused by lack of sleep.

Sleep apnea is one of the conditions that has shown us just how much deep, restful sleep our brain needs. People with sleep apnea tend to be at a high risk for heart disease and cancer, as well as increased risk for strokes.

Sleep deprivation is clearly implicated in brain atrophy. Ideally, seven to eight hours of sleep is the most optimum suggestion for adults. Teens need about nine hours of sleep per night. What teen taking typical AP high school classes gets nine hours of sleep?

When we don't get adequate sleep, it increases the cortisol levels in our brain, which increases the hyperalertness to our surroundings. This hyperalert state is one of too much arousal. Insomnia patients tend to have high levels of fast beta activity, which is an obsessive, overthinking brain.

Over time, poor sleep quality and lack of sleep has a direct effect on the structure of the brain in that it shrinks the hippocampus. Regularly interrupted sleep also causes pain syndromes such as fibromyalgia, hypertension, and general inflammation in the belly. We all tend to do worse on any tests of cognitive assessments when we are sleep-deprived.

Furthermore, the circadian rhythm is critical to the maintenance of homeostasis of the body. Our sleep cycles impact the choices we make with food. The frontal lobe of the brain, the "braking system," shows impairment in its ability when subjects are sleep-deprived.

Our gas pedal goes at full throttle when we are sleep-deprived. Food cravings tend to increase in all of us when we are sleep-deprived. The brain's restorative functions operate completely when we are asleep. Approximately fifty chemicals are renewed and rejuvenated in the brain when we sleep!

The best news is that sleep, the type of sleep, and the right quality and quantity of sleep can put the brain and body back on track. Many of the conditions seen in patients with snoring and sleep apnea are reversed when sleep issues are fixed. This is where neurofeedback is one of the most powerful treatment modalities. No matter what issues we treat at our center, sleep regulation is one of the benefits that our patients rave about in the first three weeks of treatment.

Ambien would lose its stronghold on Americans if neurofeedback became the initial treatment of choice for the brain. There are studies that have linked the usage of Ambien to cancers. Although Ambien creates sleep onset, it affects the quality of sleep.

The reduction in REM sleep means the brain does not make the chemicals to restore the body, so inflammation of the brain may be one of the places we want to look at with the onsets of cancers. Nurses who work overnight shifts have a much higher incidence of breast cancer. See the link between sleep and inflammation?

Another brain-enhancing activity that helps the onset of sleep is meditation.

Meditation

A calm, focused, and attentive mind is one that we all admire. We have met people who just seem to emanate equipoise, seem alert yet calm, listen well, and seem to be efficient by doing one thing at a time.

In this fast, social media- and technology-obsessed world we live in, we have so many distractions that charge at us all the time. Our attention spans have become shorter and shorter in these last two decades with the emergence of the Internet in our lives. As this book was being written, my brain was so distracted that I had to get away from all technology to remain focused and productive.

Video games, apps, on-demand programming, YouTube videos, and social media such as Instagram and Facebook all contrive to distance us from ourselves. More and more social scientists are writing about the disconnect we are all experiencing, as we get into a more digitalized, less emotionally connected world.

The essence of meditation is to calm the brain down. If too much stimulation is inflaming the brain, then isn't meditation the best key to balancing the CEO of our body? The simplest of meditation routines can do wonders for our brain. Doing breath meditation for five minutes increases the oxygen capacity of our brain by 80%. Can you imagine your brain receiving an upgrade of 80% with five minutes of breath work?

Meditation has been proved scientifically to grow neurons in the brain! Obviously, meditation reduces stress on the body and the brain. However, more than that, meditation increases the levels of BDNF in the brain and can increase the size of the hippocampus.

Remember a larger, more defined hippocampus means that your memory remains sharp. If memory is sharp, cognitive decline is decreased. Meditation has been proved to improve sleep function, increase immunity, reduce blood pressure, and increase blood flow to the brain. It also helps us balance emotion because it directly impacts the amygdala — the emotional center of the brain.

Attention and emotional regulation are two of the first places where meditation shows its positive impact. Meditation has been scientifically proven to increase the thickness of the cortex of the brain. The cortex of 45- to 50-year-old meditators was the same as the cortex of 20- to 30-year-olds. Meditation can drop your brain age by decades.

One study conducted by Lazar in 2011 showed that meditation increased the size of the hippocampus, posterior cingulate cortex, the temporoparietal junction, and the cerebellum. These brain regions are involved in learning and memory, emotional regulation, self-referential processing (us versus me), and perspective-taking, or resiliency. None of these changes were seen in the control group of non-meditators.

The brain's highways become super-efficient when we meditate. Keeping our "roads" running smoothly is the essence of good to excellent brain health. A therapy technique that has been able to get many brains ready for meditation is neurofeedback, which we'll look at next.

Neurofeedback

As you read this section on neurofeedback, it must be evident to you that one of the most powerful ways you can improve the structure, function, and health of your brain is through neurofeedback. The brain's electrical activity is highly measurable and now that we know specifically what regions of the brain are activated under various cognitive challenges and emotional tasks, we are able to tailor highly specific treatment protocols.

A person who wants to improve their handwriting and manual dexterity can come into neurofeedback just for that. A dancer who wants to improve his or her form will come in specifically to become better tuned with specific postures that may be particularly challenging and elusive. Neuro-feedback is particularly successful with sleep induction, so that gives us an idea of how happy the brain becomes when it receives neurofeedback.

With the myriad of factors that affect the brain from food to sleep to exercise, neurotoxins, and environmental toxins, the brain needs and deserves all the help we can give it. If we serve our brain well, then our brain will serve us for the rest of our lives. A small investment in neurofeedback can give your body distance from autoimmune conditions, cancers, diabetes, high blood pressure, and dementia.

In today's supercharged, super-fast world, our techno-logical revolution has afforded us new vistas that we never knew were possible—just as when airliners were invented, opening doors to lands we could not have traveled to before.

Neuroscientists and research scientists in the studies of illnesses and brain states are giving us a wealth of infor-mation, which we as neurotherapists are able to apply and produce tremendous growth and changes in the state of a

person's health. If there is a treatment modality that allevi-
ates stress and anxiety, helps you sleep better, and perhaps
even allow you to reduce the dosages on a number of medications, would that be a treatment you would jump for?

Brain retraining is extremely unrecognized, undervalued,
and unknown by most healthcare practitioners today. Those
of us that are daily practitioners of neurofeedback see our
patients evolving in their growth that astounds us again and
again.

As a practitioner of neurofeedback, the success stories of
our patients are so heartwarming that I want to be able to
spread the word regarding this methodology that is still so
relatively unknown. The very gift of the technological revolution has actually allowed us to create neurofeedback systems that are more technologically sophisticated, allowing
us to get better results with fewer sessions. As more researchers are conducting studies related to the successes of
neurofeedback, the medical community is taking a slow yet
intrigued peek at this highly successful treatment modality.

One of the most significant ways in which neurofeedback
is successful is in the area of memory training, which is a
powerful brain enhancer.

Memory Training and Learning New Things

Building brain muscles, just as we build our quads or biceps,
is the essence of memory training. The hippocampus is the
organ that really wants to grow, enlarge, develop, and make
friends! Practicing memorization is the *best* way to make the
cortex and hippocampus thicker.

With the advent of cell phones, we no longer memorize phone numbers. GPS devices make our life so much easier because we can get places faster without getting lost. Our brain is losing essential "workout" time periods with our overreliance on technology.

Practicing memorization is what improves the performance of our brain. At the neuronal level when we are memorizing, we are adding and strengthening synapses, neurons, and other fiber bundles in the brain. As we train the brain muscles through memorization, we are reshaping our brain so that it communicates better with all other regions of the brain.

This cognitive stimulation is known to increase blood flow to the brain as well as increase levels of BDNF to the brain. Remember, BDNF is the neurochemical that is the brain fertilizer. The type of brainwave activity also changes when we practice memorization skills, which only enhances the effects of neurofeedback.

One of the best things that any brain can do is to learn a new language. Even taking a class that teaches you a new technique of roping or jewelry-making stimulates neuronal growth in the brain. When we have engaged our brains in anything intensive such as learning a new skill, we have just given our brains a shot of BDNF. As we keep doing this, it enhances our sense of well-being. The sharper, clearer focus helps us sleep well at night, which helps us make better choices with food and exercise, with the positive benefits going on and on.

One of the disadvantages created by our information overload and overstimulated environments is that we may think we are reading a lot—however, we may just be skimming. When we are skimming, we are only using the frontal lobes, not the hippocampus. Thorough, sustained, committed-to-memory reading uses the hippocampus plus the frontal lobes. Reading thoroughly and deeply as well as practicing memorization may be the brain training that is crucial for us to delay the onset of dementia.

We all know that we tend to remember things have had an emotional linkage to them. Those of us that are baby boomers can remember exactly what we were doing when we heard that JFK was assassinated. Furthermore, with 9/11 as an event of the recent past, we have vivid memories of what we were doing when we first saw the images of the planes hitting the Twin Towers.

So, memory training becomes more efficient when we pair emotion with it. Other techniques and skills involved chunking, creating visual maps in your brain as well as really pushing the brain past the discomfort of not remembering. I am an avid supporter of Luminosity, the brain-training website where I suggest to my patients that they do fifteen minutes of cognitive training every day.

Perhaps brain enhancement is best supported by our state of mind—optimism and compassion are traits that seem to exist in supercharged, well brains that seem to have resiliency.

Optimism and Compassion

As you traverse the vast land of the brain landscape, the connection between the mind and the brain needs to be enhanced. At our clinic, one of the ways we discuss optimum health is by coaching the brain to do what the mind is hungry for. We are all working toward a state we call "happiness," with some of us finding this way of being easier to come by than others.

Many of us have this mistaken belief that we are either an optimist, pessimist, or, as some say, a realist. It is imperative that you know that even though you may consider yourself a pessimist, it is very possible to be able to change your mindset to that of an optimist.

The body and the brain are madly in love with the state of optimism. Optimism is a trait that can be cultivated with determination and effort. First you may be saying, "Why would I want to be an optimist? Those people are in la-la land. They are in the clouds and they really don't have a real picture of the suffering that is in this world."

Studies have shown that resilient, optimistic children learn *better* and *faster*. That means that there are ways in which the brain produces neurohormones and neurotransmitters when we look at the positive side of things that function as a neuroprotective factor.

Memory function is enhanced in optimistic people because they throw out less of the stress hormone, cortisol. If we have the ability to perceive events in a positive light, then our body doesn't take as much of a toll. This means that more BDNF is produced, less cortisol is produced, and the body/brain duo is happy and satisfied.

Compassion is a trait that enhances the brain in a very deep, sophisticated way. The state of compassion begs peace, calm, equanimity, and emotional generosity. When one is in a kind place with themselves, it becomes natural not to get stirred up by others. A kind, generous, compassionate heart tends to evoke feelings of warmth, which then make the person glow on the inside.

Mindfulness researchers are presenting excellent studies that are showing the effects of enhanced cortical growth in the brain as a result of three weeks of daily compassionate training. If three weeks create such a supercharged brain, then imagine how a lifetime of brain training as a practice could ward off so much brain disease.

A belief that there is goodness in the world creates a sense of joy and awe in the world. When one operates from a place of the cup being half full, we look for the goodness in others, how we can give to others, and how we can be contributing members of society. The optimism and compassion generate love and bonding hormones such as oxytocin, which fight off the combative influence of cortisol.

There are numerous studies conducted on how pessimistic people are more prone to depression and anxiety. Some of the most successful methodologies for the treatment of depression incorporate mindfulness methods such as cultivating compassion and enhancing optimism.

The single most protective factor for brain regeneration is a substance called BDNF (Brain-Derived Neurotrophic Factor), which we'll discuss next.

BDNF and Epigenetics

BDNF and epigenetics are the brain fertilizers that enhance the functioning of the neurons in our brains. New cells in the hippocampus grow because of BDNF. The healing, repairing, and replacement occur in the brain because of the presence of BDNF. The brain can only remain in peak condition if enough BDNF is produced.

BDNF also protects existing neurons, ensuring their survival while encouraging more synapses to form. This synaptic connection is vital for thinking, learning, and higher levels of brain function. Studies have shown low levels of BDNF in Alzheimer's patients. The gene that turns on BDNF fortunately is very controllable through our lifestyle choices.

Epigenetics is the process by which we can turn down the dial on our genetics. This exciting field is up and coming. We now know that we could be born with certain genetics and that our genetics do not have to be our destiny. We can actually take charge and impact our health, longevity, and wellness through substitute lifestyle factors.

Reducing inflammation in the body via vigorous exercise, quality eating, brain training, and meditation all help us take charge of our brain's destiny despite its blueprint DNA. Sugars and gluten are enemies of the brain. Alcohol consumption functions as a neurotoxin; to reduce inflammation, alcohol has to be reduced or stopped completely.

There are further epigenetic factors that can dial up the genetics. Some of these are the electromagnetic radiation from cell phones, computers, plasma TVs, and cell phone towers. As of today, we are not certain what neurogenic changes may be happening at the chromosomal levels. The damage occurring to the DNA with various kinds of oxidative stress cannot be understated. Other environmental toxins that dial up the epigenetics can be cleaners and toxins from cleaning supplies and plastics.

Modern man has certainly created enough turbulence in recent centuries to create imbalances that can threaten the quality of our lives. Inasmuch as we have advanced with science, the brain certainly will benefit from all the research that is emerging from latest science and technology. Our nemesis will create solutions for us if only we allow ourselves to utilize this knowledge to the fullest extent possible.

We hope that this book on the exciting field of neurofeedback—and how it can help you have a turbocharged brain, benefiting your work and personal life—has given you adequate knowledge, information, and tools to keep your brain healthy and fit. Neurofeedback is *the* most cutting-edge tool available that can give you an edge that far surpasses anything else. Explore brain neurogenesis with neurofeedback.

REFERENCES

American Association for the Advancement of Science. (2012). Record 4.02 billion prescriptions in United States in 2011. *American Chemical Society.* Retrieved from: https://www.eurekalert.org/pub_releases/2012-09/acs-r4b091212.php

Blakeslee, S. (2007). A small part of the brain, and its profound effects. *The New York Times.* Retrieved from: https://www.nytimes.com/2007/02/06/health/psychology/06brain.html

Boyatzis, R. E., Rochford, K., & Taylor, S. N. (2015). The role of the positive emotional attractor in vision and shared vision: toward effective leadership, relationships, and engagement. *Frontiers in Psychology, 6,* 670.

Brain Paint. (2019). Next generation neurofeedback. Retrieved from: https://neurofeedback-system.com

Centers for Disease Control. (2016). National prevalence of ADHD and Treatment: New statistics for children and adolescents. Retrieved from: https://www.cdc.gov/ncbddd/adhd/features/national-prevalence-adhd-and-treatment.html

Coben, R. & Padolsky, I. (2007). Assessment-guided neurofeedback for autistic spectrum disorder. *Journal of Neurotherapy, 11,* 5-23.

Erickson, K. I., Raji, C. A., Lopez, O. L., Becker, J. T., Rosano, C., Newman, A. B., & Kuller, L. H. (2010). Physical activity predicts gray matter volume in late adulthood:

the Cardiovascular Health Study. *Neurology, 75,* 1415–1422.

Hammond, D.C. (2011). What is neurofeedback: An update. *Journal of Neurotherapy, 15,* 305-336.

Horowitz, J.M., & Graf, N. (2019). Most U.S. teens see anxiety and depression as a major problem among their peers. *Pew Research Center.* Retrieved from: https://www.pewsocialtrends.org/2019/02/20/most-u-s-teens-see-anxiety-and-depression-as-a-major-problem-among-their-peers/

International Society for Neurofeedback and Research. (2020). Introduction to the equipment and process. Retrieved from: https://isnr.org/neurofeedback-introduction

Mack, M. G., & Ragan, B. G. (2008). Development of the mental, emotional, and bodily toughness inventory in collegiate athletes and nonathletes. *Journal of Athletic Training, 43*(2), 125–132.

Marzbani, H., Marateb, H. R., & Mansourian, M. (2016). Neurofeedback: A comprehensive review on system design, methodology and clinical applications. *Basic and Clinical Neuroscience, 7*(2), 143–158.

McGreevey, S. (2011). Meditation study shows changes associated with awareness, stress. *The Harvard Gazette.* Retrieved from: https://news.harvard.edu/gazette/story/2011/01/eight-weeks-to-a-better-brain/

Sax, L. (2017). The collapse of parenting. *Cesa 6.* Retrieved from: https://www.cesa6.org/smart_summaries/The-Collapse-of-Parenting.pdf

Search Inside Yourself Leadership Institute. (2020). Transformational experiences backed by world experts in neuroscience, mindfulness and emotional intelligence. Retrieved from: https://siyli.org

Siegel, D. (2011). Identifying your child's attachment style. *Psych Alive.* Retrieved from: https://www.psychalive.org/identifying-your-childs-attachment-style-2/

Tal, A., & Bar, M. (2014). The proactive brain and the fate of dead hypotheses. *Frontiers in Computational Neuroscience, 8,* 138.

Townsend. A. (2013). Neurofeedback helps relieve chemo brain symptoms, Cleveland researcher finds. *Cleveland.com.* Retrieved from: https://www.cleveland.com/healthfit/2013/04/neurofeedback_helps_relieve_ch.html

van der Kolk, B.A., Hodgdon, H., Gapen, M., Musicaro, R., Suvak, M.K., Hamlin, E., et al. (2016) A randomized controlled study of neurofeedback for chronic PTSD. *PLoS ONE* 11(12): e0166752. doi:10.1371/journal.pone.0166752

GLOSSARY OF BRAIN TERMS

Adrenaline: A hormone secreted by the adrenal glands, especially in conditions of stress, increasing rates of blood circulation, breathing, and carbohydrate metabolism and preparing muscles for exertion.

Alpha/Theta protocol: Alpha/Theta protocol asks the individual to recall one event that has caused distress. After that heightened arousal, we introduce Alpha/Theta training, in which we want to evoke the calming alpha waves to override the agitated high-beta waves that show up.

Alpha waves: (8–12 Hz) Alpha waves are present when your brain is in an idling default state, typically created when you're daydreaming or consciously practicing mindfulness or meditation. Alpha waves can also be created by aerobic exercise.

Amygdala: An almond-shaped set of neurons located deep in the brain's medial temporal lobe. Shown to play a key role in the processing of emotions, the amygdala forms part of the limbic system.

Anterior cingulate cortex: The front-most portion of the cingulate cortex, the anterior cingulate cortex (or ACC) has been implicated in several complex cognitive functions, such as empathy, impulse control, emotion, and decision-making.

Beta waves: (12–30 Hz) Beta waves typically dominate our normal waking states of consciousness and occur when attention is directed toward cognitive and other tasks. Beta is a "fast" wave activity that is present when we are alert, attentive, focused, and engaged in problem-solving or decision-making. Depression and anxiety have also been linked to beta waves because they can lead to "rut-like" thinking patterns.

Brain-derived neurotrophic factor: A protein that, in humans, is encoded by the BDNF gene. This protein promotes the survival of nerve cells (neurons) by playing a role in the growth, maturation (differentiation), and maintenance of these cells.

Brain training: A program of regular activities purported to maintain or improve one's cognitive abilities. The phrase "cognitive ability" usually refers to components of fluid intelligence such as executive function and working memory.

Central nervous system: Controls most functions of the body and mind. It consists of two parts: the brain and the spinal cord. The brain is the center of our thoughts, the interpreter of our external environment, and the origin of control over body movement.

Cerebellum: A major part of the hindbrain, playing an important role in motor control.

Cerebral cortex: Plays a key role in attention, perception, awareness, thought, memory, language, and consciousness.

DHA: Docosahexaenoic acid is a type of omega-3 fat. DHA may help reduce inflammation and the risk of chronic diseases, such as heart disease. DHA supports brain function and eye health.

EEG: A test used to find problems related to electrical activity of the brain. An EEG tracks and records brain wave patterns. Small metal discs with thin wires (electrodes) are placed on the scalp, and then send signals to a computer to record the results.

Epigenetics: The study of changes in organisms caused by modification of gene expression rather than alteration of the genetic code itself.

Epinephrine: A chemical that narrows blood vessels and opens airways in the lungs. These effects can reverse severe low blood pressure, wheezing, severe skin itching, hives, and other symptoms of an allergic reaction.

fMRI: Functional magnetic resonance imaging or functional MRI (fMRI) measures brain activity by detecting changes associated with blood flow. This technique relies on the fact that cerebral blood flow and neuronal activation are coupled. When an area of the brain is in use, blood flow to that region also increases.

Gamma waves: (25–100 Hz) Gamma waves typically hover around 40 Hz and are the fastest of the brain wave bandwidths. Gamma waves relate to simultaneous processing of information from different brain areas and have been associated with higher states of conscious perception.

Hippocampus: A brain structure embedded deep in the temporal lobe of each cerebral cortex. It is an important part of the limbic system, a cortical region that regulates motivation, emotion, learning, and memory.

Hypothalamus: A small region of the brain. It's located at the base of the brain, near the pituitary gland. While it's very small, the hypothalamus plays a crucial role in many important functions, including releasing hormones and regulating body temperature.

Insula: Plays a role in a variety of homeostatic functions related to basic survival needs, such as taste, visceral sensation, and autonomic control. The insula controls autonomic functions through the regulation of the sympathetic and parasympathetic systems. It has a role in regulating the immune system.

Limbic brain: A set of structures in the brain that deal with emotions and memory. It regulates autonomic or endocrine function in response to emotional stimuli and also is involved in reinforcing behavior.

Neocortex: The part of the mammalian brain involved in higher-order brain functions such as sensory perception, cognition, generation of motor commands, spatial reasoning, and language.

Neurofeedback brain training: A type of biofeedback in which neural activity is measured and presented through one or more sensory channels to the participant in real time to facilitate self-regulation.

Neuroplasticity: Also known as brain plasticity, neuro-elasticity, or neural plasticity, is the ability of the brain to change continuously throughout an individual's life.

Neurotransmitter: A chemical substance that is released at the end of a nerve fiber by the arrival of a nerve impulse and, by diffusing across the synapse or junction, causes the transfer of the impulse to another nerve fiber, a muscle fiber, or some other structure.

Norepinephrine: Also called noradrenaline, a substance that is released predominantly from the ends of sympathetic nerve fibers. It acts to increase the force of skeletal muscle contraction and the rate and force of contraction of the heart.

Orbital frontal cortex: A prefrontal cortex region in the frontal lobes of the brain that is involved in the cognitive process of decision-making.

Oxytocin: A peptide hormone and neuropeptide. It is normally produced in the hypothalamus and released by the posterior pituitary. It plays a role in social bonding, sexual reproduction, childbirth, and the period after childbirth.

Parasympathetic nervous system: One of three divisions of the autonomic nervous system. Sometimes called the rest and digest system, the parasympathetic system conserves energy as it slows the heart rate, increases intestinal and gland activity, and relaxes sphincter muscles in the gastrointestinal tract.

Pituitary gland: A pea-sized gland that is housed within a bony structure (*sella turcica*) at the base of the brain. The *sella turcica* protects the pituitary but allows very little room for expansion. The pituitary controls the function of most other endocrine glands and is therefore sometimes called the master gland.

Prefrontal cortex: The cerebral cortex covering the front part of the frontal lobe. This brain region has been implicated in planning complex cognitive behavior, personality expression, decision-making, and moderating social behavior.

REM sleep: A kind of sleep that occurs at intervals during the night and is characterized by rapid eye movements, more dreaming and bodily movement, and faster pulse and breathing.

Serotonin: Low serotonin levels have been linked to depression. Serotonin is an important chemical and neurotransmitter in the human body. It is believed to help regulate mood and social behavior, appetite and digestion, sleep, memory, and sexual desire and function.

Sympathetic nervous system: Directs the body's rapid involuntary response to dangerous or stressful situations. A flash flood of hormones boosts the body's alertness and heart rate, sending extra blood to the muscles.

Thalamus: A small structure within the brain located just above the brain stem between the cerebral cortex and the midbrain and has extensive nerve connections to both. The main function of the thalamus is to relay motor and sensory signals to the cerebral cortex.

Theta waves: (3–8 Hz) Theta waves occur during sleep but have also been observed in the deepest states of Zen meditation.

Trichotillomania: Also referred to as the "hair-pulling disorder," trichotillomania is a mental disorder classified under obsessive-compulsive and related disorders. It involves recurrent, irresistible urges to pull hair from the scalp, eyebrows, eyelids, and other areas of the body.

APPENDIX:
RESOURCES FOR NEUROFEEDBACK

Choosing a Neurotherapist

According to the Association for Applied Psychophysiology and Biofeedback (AAPB), most states do not restrict who can perform biofeedback services. As such, any person without clinical training or specialized training in biofeedback may claim to provide biofeedback services.

When choosing a neurotherapist, the only way to have assurance about the provider is to review their formal training in the biofeedback type needed to treat your problem, and their training in assessment and treatment of your problem. The AAPB strongly recommends that anyone providing biofeedback sources should at least meet the minimum standards of knowledge, training, and experience required to be certified by the Biofeedback Certification International Alliance (BCIA). One should be very cautious if the provider is not certified by the BCIA. You can find providers by looking at the practitioner directory sections of the AAPB and BCIA, seen in the links below.

- https://www.aapb.org/i4a/memberDirectory/index .cfm?directory_id=4&pageID=3834

- https://certify.bcia.org/4dcgi/resctr/search.html

Each provider has a designation specific to their certification. BCB describes professionals certified in general biofeedback such as SEMG, Thermal, GSR, HRV, and an overview of neurofeedback. BCN signifies professionals certified in neurofeedback or EEG neurofeedback. BCB-PMD professionals are certified to use SEMG biofeedback to treat elimination disorders such as incontinence and pelvic pain.

Book Recommendations

In *Brain Wars*, acclaimed neuroscientist Mario Beauregard reveals compelling new evidence set to provoke a major shift in our understanding of the mind-body debate: research showing that the mind and consciousness are transmitted and filtered through the brain—but are not generated by it.

Beauregard, M. (2012). *Brain Wars*. New York, NY: Harper Collins.

Science writer Jim Robbins suggests that some such conditions—such as epilepsy, autism, and depression—could yield to a recently developed technique called neurofeedback. His book *A Symphony in the Brain* describes the process, its evolution from the 1970s fad of biofeedback, its practitioners, and some of its success stories. Using computers to quickly provide information on real-time EEGs, practitioners train patients to control global or local brain states—or so the theory goes.

Robbins, J. (2014). *A symphony in the brain: The evolution of the new brain wave biofeedback*. New York, NY: Grove Press.

Evidence-Based Practice in Biofeedback and Neurofeedback (3rd ed.) is the most comprehensive review of research in the field of neurofeedback and biofeedback available to clinicians. Perhaps the most important aspect of this review is the ranking of the studies for each disorder based on the methodological quality of the research.

Tan, G., Shaffer, F., Lyle, R., Teo, I., & Lyle R. (2016). *Evidence-based practice in biofeedback and neurofeedback 3rd edition*. Wheat Ridge, CO: AAPB.

Internet Resources

The Association for Applied Psychophysiology and Biofeedback, Inc. (AAPB) provides texts on biofeedback as well as news, continuing education, and information on finding a practitioner.

- https://www.aapb.org

The Biofeedback Certification International Alliance is an organization that certifies individuals who meet the education and training standards in biofeedback and those who advance their knowledge through continuing education.

- https://www.bcia.org

EEG Info is a website dedicated to neurofeedback education and has many articles by doctors at the EEG Institute. Its website hosts many links on the application and mechanisms of brain self-regulation that underline neurofeedback.

- https://www.eeginfo.com/research/

The International Society for Neurofeedback and Research is a premier membership organization that promotes neurofeedback. Its website hosts a comprehensive bibliography that shows relevant research according to diagnosis.

- https://isnr.org/interested-professionals/
  recommended-reading

In this article, the *San Diego Union-Tribune* speaks with Dr. Divya Kakaiya about neurofeedback and the ways in which the treatment enhances brain neurocircuitry. She describes her personal mission for people to be more aware of non-medical treatments for depression, anxiety, ADHD, and addiction.

- https://www.sandiegouniontribune.com/lifestyle/people/sd-utbg-someone-san-diego-know-kakaiya-20190304-story.html

Dr. Divya Kakaiya speaks with Bev and Heather of the *Bitches Be Brave* podcast available on Spotify. She discusses the environmental factors that affect our brains, including technology and the increase in ADHD since the launch of the iPhone, iPad, and similar technology.

- https://open.spotify.com/episode/6ONAz14XHcnq7qZN9bEs5I

Dr. Divya Kakaiya speaks with Dr. Christine Horner about her organization, "Healthy Within," a state-of-the-art integrative brain health and wellness center. In this two-part interview, Dr. Kakaiya speaks about the effectiveness of neurofeedback in healing conditions such as depression, insomnia, ADHD, anxiety, and post-concussive syndrome.

- https://www.iheart.com/podcast/966-the-radiant-health-29061929/episode/divya-kakaiya-optimizing-brain-health-29191242/

Healthy Within is an integrative brain health and psychological wellness center that offers treatment for depression, anxiety, obsessive compulsive disorder, parent–teen issues, family conflict, attention deficit disorder, cultural issues, sexual trauma, alcoholism/substance abuse, post-traumatic stress disorder, traumatic brain injuries, stroke, and dementia. Founded by Dr. Divya Kakaiya in 1999, Healthy Within strives to use the power of non-medical treatment to enhance the brain and mind.

- https://healthywithin.com

D.C. Hammond provides an article that describes the overview of the field of neurofeedback (EEG biofeedback), as well as an update on the research. Hammond explains the process of assessment and neurofeedback training. Then, areas in which neurofeedback is being used as a treatment are identified and research findings are presented. Hammond also describes potential risks and side effects as well as guidelines for selecting a qualified practitioner

Hammond, D. C. (2011). What is neurofeedback: An update. *Journal of Neurotherapy, 15,* 305-336.

In a study by van der Kolk and colleagues (2016), researchers found that brain/computer interaction devices alter neural signals and mental activity. Using EEG neurofeedback training in patients with chronic PTSD, the PTSD symptoms were reduced, while there was an increase in the capacity to regulate affect.

- http://www.traumacenter.org/products/pdf_files/ Randomized_Controlled_Study_Neurofeedback_ Chronic_PTSD_V0002.pdf

van der Kolk, B.A., Hodgdon, H., Gapen, M., Musicaro, R., Suvak, M.K., Hamlin, E., et al. (2016) A randomized controlled study of neurofeedback for chronic PTSD. *PLoS ONE* 11(12): e0166752. doi:10.1371/journal. pone.0166752

ACKNOWLEDGMENTS

DEEP, DEEP APPRECIATION to my daughter, Dr. Roshni Kakaiya, who has been instrumental in helping me with reads and re-reads of my manuscript. She has an eye for detail that amazes and delights me. She is a family medicine doctor who had worked at Healthy Within before medical school, and knows firsthand the power of neurofeedback and cannot wait to have it at her clinic.

And of course, we know this field of neurofeedback that I am in would not be possible if it was not for Kush's gifted brain. My son, Kush, has taught me so much about how to be a mom who can learn and grow from her child. He was my beacon of light that brought me into this world.

Kush and Roshni, thank you to both of you for reminding me not to give up on this project ... and always being excited for me when I picked the book up again! I could not have completed this passion project if you both had not encouraged me!

Cory Emberson, you were a Godsend to me at the right time, and your attention to detail and the positive, light, encouraging notes made a world of difference for me. You deconstructed the process so well, and for that I will remain eternally grateful.

Even though we did not formally partner, Kelly Shetron, our conversations sparked a desire in me to have my passion heard. Thank you for probing so deeply, asking me the right questions, and allowing me to believe that we can make a *huge* difference! Maybe we will collaborate on my next book!

Carl and Andi Kosnar, you both came into my life and gave neurofeedback the rebirth it *so* needed by helping me convert what I do into a franchise. Your guidance and support are invaluable. Michael Lindsay, our attorney, believed so much in the healing power of neurofeedback that he was not going to give up until we got approval from the State of California. The three of you are my "A" team!

The deepest debt of gratitude I owe is to my patients, who for the last 35 years have trusted me, and have shared their darkest sources of pain with me. My gift as a healer can only be realized if the folks who come and share "our" intimate space teach me how to support them so that the brain, mind, and body can heal. Hope and healing are the hallmarks of Healthy Within.

EPILOGUE

THE TIME OF PUBLICATION OF THIS BOOK is extremely auspicious, since at the exact time that this book is going to print is when we are on the brink of selling our neurofeedback franchises.

I have a dream…

My dream is to have neurofeedback become a household word like coffee, tea, yoga, or, heaven forbid, Prozac.

My dream is to have commercials for neurofeedback that replace all the medication commercials that we are inundated with on TV.

My dream is to have empathy in the world, and neurofeedback directly creates empathy by rewiring the brain.

My dream is to have compassion in the world. When we do right-side training with neurofeedback, we increase empathy in that person.

My dream is to have at least 50 Healthy Withins in every state.

My dream is to have Healthy Within Neurofeedback Centers all over the world!

It is possible and we are on our way.

Healthy Within Neurofeedback *will* become a household word!

INDEX